More Weekend Crochet Projects

Margaret Hubert
Dorothy Gusick

 VAN NOSTRAND REINHOLD COMPANY
New York Cincinnati Toronto London Melbourne

To our families

Printed in the United States of America

Designed by Charlotte Staub
Photographs by Stephen E. Morton

Published by Van Nostrand Reinhold Company Inc.
135 West 50th Street
New York, New York 10020

Van Nostrand Reinhold
480 Latrobe Street
Melbourne, Victoria 3000, Australia

Van Nostrand Reinhold Company Limited
Molly Millars Lane
Wokingham, Berkshire RG11 2PY, England

16 15 14 13 12 11 10 9 8 7 6 5 4 3 2 1

Library of Congress Cataloging in Publication Data
Hubert, Margaret.
    More weekend crochet projects.
    Includes index.
    1. Crocheting. I. Gusick, Dorothy. II. Title.
TT820.H839 1983   746.43'4041   83-3563
ISBN 0-442-23247-0

contents

acknowledgments

We wish to thank everyone that helped make this book possible. Special thanks to Susan Rosenthal Gies, our editor, Nancy N. Green, editor-in-chief at Van Nostrand Reinhold, Stephen E. Morton, our photographer, Mary Aleide, Caroline Ambrosino, Florence Greges, and Minnie Grippo who helped crochet many of the garments.

Last but not least, a special thanks to each and every one of the models:

Priscilla Albrecht
Donna Baldassare
Camile Bracco
Cori Chu
Lisa Ciero
Keith Cobb
Pam Cobb
Bernadette Czarniecki
Cari DeLucci
Donna Duggan
Jean Duggan

Stacy Federico
Philip J. Federico
Erica Fredrickson
Susan Fuirst
Natalie Gaitas
Matthew Gardner
David Gusick
Robert Gusick
Chris Hubert
Eric Hubert
Grace Hubert

Mark Hubert
Robert M. Hubert
Celeste Lawler
Karen Ludwig
Mary Theresa Martin
Robert Martin
Dorothy McGinty
Julie Rosenthal
Scott Strauss
Michelle Schierenberg

introduction

For many years the popular conception of crochet was limited to intricate lacy doilies, tablecloths, bedspreads, and antimacassars. These household items were worked with fine white or ecru thread and a very small hook. Today, although we marvel at the infinite care and patience that it took to create these beautiful heirlooms, very few of us have the spare time to attempt to make these things. We believe that today's busy woman would enjoy creating smart-looking, stylish sweaters and accessories even though the time that she is able to devote to these projects may be quite limited. Most of the items that we have included in this book can be made in a weekend.

We hope to demonstrate how even a novice can turn out fashionable garments and accessories, as well as household items, quickly and easily. In most cases we have used very basic stitches to make the articles in this book. Great-looking effects can be achieved by using interesting textured yarns and imaginative color combinations. Before beginning a project, "play" with the yarn. See how the colors and textures work together when they are held and twisted in your hands. We have been delighted with some of the wonderful and unexpected mixes that emerged from leftovers in our yarn basket. We have even used seam binding for a woman's vest and set of placemats, as well as household twine for another placemat project.

With the resurgence of interest in beautiful handmade clothing, many high-fashion designers are showing hand-knitted and crocheted sweaters in their collections. In this book we have designed many smart-looking garments for men, women, and children. We hope that the style-conscious crocheter will enjoy creating these lovely items—all, in a very short time.

4

In working with very bulky yarns (or two strands of yarn held together) and with very large crochet hooks, it is necessary to incorporate a few tips or to bend the rules occasionally. The following tips will help you out.

• When sewing seams, hold pieces to be sewn together on a flat surface and weave the seams with a close back-and-forth stitch. This will make a very flat seam.

• Never block heavily textured crochet. It will flatten your stitches and make your work appear lifeless.

• When working with two or more strands of yarn, it is helpful to put each yarn in a separate bag. Keeping skeins separate as you work will prevent tangles, will allow you to work at a faster pace, and will eliminate frazzled nerves also.

• These garments are designed to be made quickly with a minimum of finishing. Do not be afraid to experiment a little, changing patterns or colors to create your own look.

• It is fun and rewarding to create your own look by combining yarns and colors. Just be sure that whatever yarn you choose meets the same gauge as specified in the directions or the garment will not fit properly. No matter how beautiful, if the fit is not right, your efforts will be wasted.

• Sometimes it is necessary to change the size hook that you are using in order to get the proper gauge. If you crochet loosely, use a smaller size hook; if you crochet tightly, use a larger size hook.

• If you are going to alter the directions in any way—by changing sleeve lengths, body lengths or pattern, etc.—be sure that you adjust your yarn purchase accordingly.

• When the directions tell you to slip stitch over a specified number of stitches and work to within a specified number of stitches, then chain and turn, these stitches are to be considered as bound-off and are not to be worked again.

• The best way to set in crocheted sleeves is to pin in sleeves first, being sure to center top of cap on shoulder seam, then start sewing at the underarm, rounding out cap as you sew in place.

• It is a good idea to pin the entire garment together before sewing. We have discovered that hair roller pins are great for pinning bulky crochet garments together. They are soft plastic, easy to use. They stay in place, are inexpensive, and can be found in most drug or variety stores.

• Even if you have been using the yarn double strand, use only one strand for sewing.

• In most cases a bulky yarn may be substituted for a double strand. Just be sure to check gauge.

• You will note that on these garments there is no shoulder shaping on back. Because of their bulkiness we find it easier to sew together along a straight line. Just pin the fronts in place and the shoulder line will form itself.

• To determine the correct size for a crocheted garment, take body measurements at the fullest part of chest, hips, and waistline. Allowances have been made for ease and proper fit. Use the size that is nearest to the chest measurement. Other adjustments may be made as you work, if necessary. Refer to chart below.

Infants' and Toddlers' Sizes

	6 mos	1	2	3	4
Chest:	19	20	21	22	23
Waist:	20	19½	20	20½	21
Hips:	20	21	22	23	24
Height:	22	25	29	31	33

Children's Sizes

	4	6	8	10	12	14
Chest:	23	24	26	28	30	32
Waist:	21	22	23½	24½	25½	26½
Hips:	24	26	28	30	32	34

Teen Boys' or Girls' Sizes

	8	10	12	14	16	18	20
Chest:	28	29	31	33	34	36	38
Waist:	23	24	25	26	29	31	33
Hips:	31	32	34	36	38	39	40

Women's Sizes

	8	10	12	14	16	18
Chest:	31½	32½	34	36	38	40
Waist:	23	24	25½	27	29	31
Hips:	33½	34½	36	38	40	42

Men's Sizes

	34	36	38	40	42	44	46
Chest:	34	36	38	40	42	44	46
Waist:	30	32	34	36	38	40	42

the language of crochet

The terms that follow are important parts of a crocheter's vocabulary. The list will serve as a crash course for the novice and as a refresher course for the more experienced crocheter.

Backward single crochet: Worked the same way as regular single crochet, but the work in *not* turned at the end of the row; rather the stitches are worked in reverse.

Battle jacket: A short jacket, with a deep, body-hugging border at waistline.

Brackets [ ] : Used to help you keep track of how many of a particular type stitch has been made and to enclose a description of a term just used.

Cap of sleeve: Describes the portion of the sleeve from the underarm to the shoulder.

Cap sleeve: A type of sleeve that covers just a small portion of the upper arm.

Cardigan: A type of garment that opens down the front and uses a zipper or buttons for closing.

Chanel jacket: A short straight jacket, falling loosely from the underarms to about 2 inches below the waist.

Cowl neck: A loose, high collar that is folded in half, draping into a soft ring around the neck.

Decrease: Unless otherwise specified, this means to draw up a loop in each of two stitches, then work it off as one stitch.

Double crochet: Yarn over hook once, pick up a loop in the next stitch, yarn over hook and draw through two loops, yarn over hook and draw through the two remaining loops.

Fringe: To make a fringe wrap yarn twice around a piece of cardboard that is about 1 inch (2.5 cm) longer than desired length of the finished fringe. Using a crochet hook, pull folded piece of yarn through one end of work about 1 inch, then pull ends through the loop and knot. Strands of yarn may be doubled or tripled for thicker fringes. Trim to even off.

Gigot sleeve: A long sleeve that fits tightly up to the elbow, then has a big, full puff from the elbow to shoulder.

Half double crochet: Yarn over hook, pick up a loop in the next stitch, yarn over hook and pull through all three loops at once.

Increase: Unless otherwise specified, this means to work two stitches into one stitch. When beginning a row, your chain always counts as the first stitch. To increase at the beginning of a row, make your chain, then also make a stitch in the first stitch instead of skipping the first stitch, as would normally be the case.

Joining yarn: Tie a knot and leave long ends that can later be woven into seams. This is best done at the outside edges of the garment. Do not ruin a garment by having an ugly knot poking through the center of your work.

Kimono sleeve: A long, loose sleeve that is straight and just as wide at the bottom as it is at the upper arm.

Loden jacket: A loosely fitting outerwear jacket that is very long and usually has frog closings instead of buttonholes.

One-piece crocheting: This can be a raglan sleeve made from the top down or a T top. The term refers to garments that include sleeve and body in one, so that there is very little or no seaming necessary.

Parentheses ( ): Used to enclose the amount of stitches required for different sizes of the garment being worked.

Pick up stitches: Refers to making new stitches that are not part of the piece being worked. For example, you might pick up stitches along a neckline, along the top of a border, or along the side of a garment.

Picot edge: Work a picot edging along a finished edge as follows: Chain 3, make 1 single crochet in the base of the chain-3, skip 1 stitch, and make a single crochet in the next stitch. Repeat all across edge.

Pierrot collar: A big ruffle collar that encircles the neck, much like a clown's ruffle.

Pom-pom: To make a pom-pom, wind yarn about 150 times around a 2-inch (5-cm) piece of cardboard. Slip yarn off cardboard and tie securely in center. Cut each end, shake vigorously, and trim to form a round ball.

Pullover: Any garment that is made without a front opening must be pulled over the head.

Raglan sleeve: A loose-fitting sleeve that is worked from the armhole up to the neck on the diagonal, rather than being set in as a conventional sleeve.

Saddle shoulder sleeve: This sleeve has a little tab at the end of the cap that fits into the shoulder line, forming a little saddle between the back and front sections of the garment.

Shawl collar: A big, turned-back collar that wraps the back of the neck and forms a V shape in front. It can be made for a pullover or a cardigan.

Single crochet: Pick up a stitch, yarn over hook, pull through both loops on hook.

Slip stitch: Pick up a loop in the next stitch, then pull the same loop through the stitch on hook.

Triple crochet: Yarn over hook twice, pick up a loop in the next stitch, yarn over hook and draw through two loops, yarn over hook and draw through two more loops, yarn over hook and draw through remaining two loops.

T top: A garment made with the sleeves as part of the body in the shape of a T.

Turtleneck: A high, close-fitting collar that hugs the neck snugly. It is usually made about 6 inches (15 cm) high, then folded in half.

Twisted cord: To make a twisted cord for a belt or a bag handle, take several strands of yarn that are five times the desired finished length, fold them in half, anchoring the folded end over a hook (or have someone hold it for you). Now twist the strands over and over until they are very tightly twisted. Being careful not to release, bring your end up to the anchored end. Hold both ends together and release center section. The strands will twist around to form a beautiful cord. Tie both ends very securely.

V neck: A neckline that forms a V shape in front. It can be made for a cardigan or a pullover.

Yarn over: Wrap yarn around hook, forming another loop on hook.

8

multicolored afghan

Every one loves an afghan, especially on a cold winter night. This beautiful bulky afghan, done in an ombré yarn with bright vibrant colors, is not only a joy under which to cuddle, but a joy to make, as well. It is crocheted in single crochet from the back loop; the yarn itself forms the interesting striping. Add a thick fringe for a dramatic effect.

Size
60 × 72 inches (152 by 183 cm)

Materials
11 skeins (8 oz or 226.8 g each) Ambrosia by Tahki, or any bulky variegated yarn to give gauge

Hook   Gauge
Size P   8 stitches = 6 inches (15 cm)

Body of Afghan
Chain 81 stitches loosely.
Foundation row: Work 1 single crochet in 2nd chain from hook, 1 single crochet in each stitch across row.
Row 1: Chain 1 to turn, skip first single crochet, make 1 single crochet from back loop in each stitch to end of row.
  Repeat row 1 till 72 inches (183 cm), end off.

Finishing
To make fringe: Cut a piece of cardboard 10 inches (25 cm) long. Wrap yarn about 20 times around cardboard. Cut one end only. Take 2 strands of yarn just cut, fold in half. Using crochet hook, pull the 2 strands through a stitch on bottom of afghan, forming a loop about 1 inch (2.5 cm), then draw loose ends through loop. Continue to wrap yarn and fringe in every other stitch along top and bottom of blanket, using 2 strands for each fringe. Do not block.

9

woman's chanel jacket

Women's Sizes
Directions are for small size. Changes for medium and large sizes are in parentheses.

Materials
6 (7, 7) skeins (3½ oz or 100 g each) Germantown Knitting Worsted by Brunswick, or any knitting worsted to give gauge
2 large buttons

Hooks
Size 10½ or K
Size N

Gauge
1 pattern sequence = 1 inch (2.5 cm)

Note: Yarn is used double strand throughout.

Back
With larger hook, chain 37 (39, 40).
Foundation row: Starting in 2nd chain from hook, *make 1 single crochet, chain 1, 1 single crochet all in same stitch, skip 1 stitch, repeat from * across row, ending with 1 single crochet in last chain.
Row 1: Chain 1 to turn, skip first stitch, *make 1 single crochet, chain 1, 1 single crochet all in next single crochet [this is first single crochet in cluster from row below], skip chain-1 and next single crochet, repeat from * across row, ending with 1 single crochet in last stitch.

Continue to repeat row 1 till 14 (14½, 15) inches (35, 36.3, 37.5 cm) from beginning. Slip stitch over 2 (2, 3) stitches, work to within 2 (2, 3) stitches of other side, chain 1, and turn. Continuing to keep pattern as established, decrease 1 stitch each side, every other row, 2 times. Work even till armhole is 7 (7½, 8) inches (17.5, 18.8, 20 cm), end off.

Left Front
Chain 20 (22, 24). Work same as for back to armhole. Shape arm side same as for back. Keep front edges even, work till armhole is 5 (5½, 6) inches (12.5, 13.8, 15 cm).

Shape neck as follows: At neck edge, slip stitch over 7 stitches, then decrease 1 stitch neck edge, every row, 2 (3, 3) times. Work even on remaining stitches to shoulder, end off.

Right Front
Work same as for left front, reversing all shaping.

Sleeves
Chain 20 (22, 24). Work pattern same as for back, increasing 1 stitch each side, every 5 inches (12.5 cm), 3 times. Being sure to form new pattern sequence as stitches are increased, work even till sleeve measures 15½ (16, 17) inches (38.8, 40, 41.3 cm) or ½ inch (1.25 cm) less than desired finished length. Slip stitch over 2 (2, 3) stitches, work to within 2 (2, 3) stitches of other side, chain 1, and turn. Continuing in pattern, decrease 1 stitch each side, every other row, 6 (7, 8) times, end off.

Easy to make, an interesting stitch, an easy fit, and an unusual two-button closing—all add up to a great little jacket. Make one for yourself or a special friend.

Finishing

Sew shoulders. Sew underarm seams. Sew sleeves and set in. With right side facing you, using smaller hook and starting at bottom right seam, work 1 row single crochet around entire outside edge of garment, making 3 single crochets in each corner to turn. When you are back to where you started, join with a slip stitch. Do not break yarn, do not turn. Work single crochet backwards over stitches just made, making 1 stitch in each stitch all around, end off. Work same trim around bottom of sleeves. Using smaller hook, make a chain 30 inches (75 cm) long. Sew 1 button in place on right front. Fold chain in half and sew it under the button, leaving 2 loose ends hanging. Sew other button in place on left front. To close garment, wrap loose strands twice around left button, and leave ends hanging. Do not block.

man's ski sweater

The interesting yoke on this man's ski sweater is made by working single crochets from the back loop and picking up stitches from several rows below. Although not a beginner's project, it can be made rather quickly because of the bulky yarn and large hook that are used.

Men's Sizes
Directions are for size 38. Changes for size 40 and 42 are in parentheses.

Materials
10 (11, 12) skeins (3½ oz or 100 g each) Vail Homespun by Brunswick—6 (7, 8) skeins in Main Color, 2 skeins each in Colors A and B—or any bulky yarn to give gauge

Hooks
Size 10½ or K
Size P

Gauge
2 stitches = 1 inch (2.5 cm)

Note: Borders and yoke are worked in single crochet from the back loop; body and sleeves are worked in single crochet from both loops.

Back
With smaller hook and Main Color, chain 10.
Foundation row: Make 1 single crochet in 2nd chain from hook, 1 single crochet in each stitch across row [9 single crochets].
Row 1: Chain 1 to turn, skip first stitch [chain-1 counts as first stitch], make 1 single crochet from back loop in next stitch, make 1 single crochet from back loop in each stitch across row.
  Repeat row 1 for 40 (42, 44) rows [20 (21, 22) ridges]. Working along

12

long edge of border, work 1 single crochet in each row [40 (42, 44) single crochets]. Change to larger hook, chain 1, turn. Continue to work in single crochet (from both loops), working 1 more row in Main Color, 2 rows in Color A, 2 rows in Color B, then finishing with Main Color till back is 14 (14½, 15) inches (35, 36.3, 37.5 cm) from the beginning, or desired length to underarm, set aside.

Front

Work same as for back to underarm, set aside.

Sleeves

With smaller hook, chain 10. Work foundation row and row 1 same as for back. Repeat row 1 for 20 (22, 24) rows. Working in single crochet along long edge of border, pick up 1 stitch in each row [20, (22, 24) single crochets]. Change to larger hook, work in pattern same as for back, increasing 1 stitch each side, every 2 inches (5 cm), 5 times. Work even till sleeve is 17 (17½, 18) inches (42.5, 43.8, 45 cm), or desired length to underarm, set aside.

Yoke

Foundation row (joining row): Using Main Color, join yarn at top of left sleeve, work single crochet from back loop across top of this sleeve, tie a colored thread in work to mark for decreases, continue across front, tie colored thread, continue across right sleeve, tie a colored thread, continue across back, tie a colored thread, join with a slip stitch to first stitch [all sections are now joined and you are ready to begin yoke]. [There should be 140 (148, 156) stitches on yoke.]
Row 1: With Main Color, work single crochet, decreasing 1 stitch before and after each marker [8 decreases made].
Row 2: With Color A, *work 3 single crochets, then work 1 long single crochet [*to make a long single crochet*: put hook into 3rd row below, draw up a long loop, then complete as a single crochet], skip next single crochet [the long single crochet has been made in its place], repeat from * all around, join with slip stitch to first stitch made.
Row 3: With Color A, work in single crochet, decreasing 1 stitch before and after each marker [8 decreases made].
Row 4: With Color B, repeat row 2.
Row 5: With Color B, repeat row 3.
Row 6: With Main Color, repeat row 2.
Row 7: With Main Color, repeat row 3.
Repeat rows 2 through 7 twice. Then repeat rows 3–6 for size 38. Repeat rows 2–7 for size 40. Repeat rows 2–7 then repeat rows 3 and 4 for size 42 [there will be 44 stitches left on neck for all sizes], end off.

Finishing

To make neckband: With smaller hook in Main Color, chain 6. Work foundation row and row 1 same as for back. Repeat row 1 for 40 (42, 44) rows, end off. Using Main Color, work 1 row single crochet around neckline, then stitch neck border in place. Sew underarm seams. Do not block.

child's sailor pullover

Children's Sizes
Directions are for size 2. Changes for sizes 4 and 6 are in parentheses.

Materials
2 skeins (3½ oz or 100 g each) Red Heart 4-ply Knitting Worsted by Coats & Clark—2 skeins in Main Color and a small amount in Color A—or any knitting worsted to give gauge

Hooks
Size 8 or H
Size 10½ or K

Gauge
2 stitches = 1 inch (2.5 cm)

Back
With smaller hook, using Main Color, chain 10.
Foundation row: Work 1 single crochet from back loop in 2nd chain from hook, 1 single crochet from back loop in each stitch to end of row [9, (9, 9) single crochets].
Row 1: Chain 1 to turn, skip first stitch [chain-1 counts as first stitch], make 1 single crochet from back loop in each stitch to end of row.

Repeat row 1 for 38 (40, 42) rows [19 (20, 21) ridges], do not break yarn. Change to larger hook, and working along side edge, pick up 1 single crochet in each row [38 (40, 42) stitches]. Chain 2 to turn, make 1 single crochet in 2nd stitch from hook, *make 1 double crochet in next stitch, 1 single crochet, repeat from * across row, chain 2 to turn.

Repeat the last row, working 2 rows of Color A, 2 rows of Main Color, 2 rows of Color A, then continuing in Main Color till 10 (10½, 11) inches (25, 25.3, 27.5 cm), or desired length to underarm. Slip stitch across 3 stitches, work pattern to within 3 stitches of other side, chain 1, and turn. Being sure to keep pattern as established, decrease 1 stitch each side, every row, 2 times. Work even till armhole is 5½ (6, 6½) inches (13.8, 15, 16.3 cm), end off.

Front
Work same as for back till armhole. Start armhole shaping same as for back, and at the same time, divide work in half, and work on left side only. Shape arm side same as for back, and at the same time, decrease 1 stitch at neck edge, every other row, till 6 (8, 8) stitches remain. Work to shoulder, end off. Join yarn and work right side to correspond, reversing all shaping.

Sleeves
With smaller hook, using Main Color, chain 10. Work same as for back for 22 rows. Change to larger hook and pick up 24 stitches along side edge. Work in pattern, increasing 1 stitch each side, every 2 inches (7.5 cm), 2 (3, 4) times. Work even till sleeve is 9 (10, 11) inches (22.5, 25, 27.5 cm), or desired length to underarm. Slip stitch over 3 stitches, work to within 3 stitches of other side, then, continuing in pattern, decrease 1 stitch each side, every row, 6 (7, 8) times. Work 1 (1, 2) row(s) even, then work 2 stitches together all across next row, end off.

A perky sailor collar and crisp contrasting color stripes make this little pullover something special. It's sure to be a favorite among boys and girls alike.

Collar

Using Main Color and larger hook, chain 22 (24, 26). Work same pattern as back for 4 rows. Continuing in pattern, work over 4 stitches, chain 1, and turn. Working on these 4 stitches only, work 4 rows, then decrease 1 stitch on inside edge, every other row, till 1 stitch remains, end off. Skipping center 17 (19, 21) stitches, join yarn at other side, and work over last 4 stitches. Work to correspond to other side, reversing shaping.

Collar Trim

Row 1: With larger hook, using Color A, and starting at bottom right point, work 1 row single crochet around outside edge of collar, making 3 single crochets in each corner.

Row 2: Using Color A, chain 1, turn, increase 1 stitch in first stitch, make 1 stitch in each stitch to corner, make 3 single crochets in corner stitch, make 1 stitch in each stitch to 2nd corner, make 3 single crochets in corner, continue down other side, increasing 1 stitch in last stitch.

Row 3 and 4: Using Main Color, repeat rows 1 and 2.

Row 5: Using Color A, repeat row 2.

Row 6: Using Color A, do not turn, work single crochet backwards all around outside edge of collar.

Inset Piece for Collar

Using larger hook and Color A, chain 12. Work single crochet for 10 (12, 14) rows, do not turn, work 1 row single crochet backwards, end off.

Finishing

Sew shoulders, sew underarm seams, set in sleeves. With right side facing wrong side of garment, pin center of collar to center back of neck. Pin points so that they meet at V shaping. Baste before sewing in place. Tack inset in place. Do not block.

The unique puff stitch combined with soft, fluffy mohair yarn give this stole a very special look. Even the most hard-to-please person on your gift list will just love it.

Women's Sizes
Approximately 20 by 62 inches (50 by 155 cm)

Materials
14 skeins (1²/₅ oz or 40 g each) Samida by Melrose, or any mohair to give gauge

Hook   **Gauge**
Size 10½ or K   1 puff stitch = 1 inch (2.5 cm)

Note: This pattern must be worked very loosely.

Body of Stole

Chain 69 very loosely to measure 21 inches (52.5 cm).

Foundation row: Make 2 double crochets in 3rd chain from hook, *skip 2 chains, make 2 double crochets in next chain, repeat from * across row, ending with 1 double crochet in the last chain [22 groups of double crochet].

Row 1: Chain 3, make 1 double crochet in 2nd double crochet of first group, chain 3, make 1 puff stitch over the bar of the double crochet just made [*to make a puff stitch*; (yarn over and pick up a long loop) 3 times, picking up the loops from right to left under the bars of double crochets, yarn over and through all but last loop, yarn over and through remaining 2]. *Skip 1 double crochet, double crochet in 2nd double crochet of group, chain 3, make 1 puff stich over bar of double crochet just made, repeat from * across row, ending with 1 double crochet in top of turning chain.

Row 2: Chain 3, turn, *make 2 double crochets in chain-3 space on top of puff stitch of row below, repeat from * across row, end 1 double crochet in top of turning chain.

Repeat rows 1 and 2 for 62 inches (155 cm), end off.

Finishing

Fringe each short end of stole.

To make fringe: Cut a piece of cardboard about 14 inches (35 cm) long. Wrap yarn around cardboard about 20 times. Cut one end only. Fold 3 strands in half. Using your crochet hook, pull looped end of strands through a stitch along edge about 1 inch (2.5 cm), then pull loose ends through loop. Continue to wrap yarn and pull through 3 strands at a time all along edge, cutting as needed.

Do not block.

This soft, fluffy little vest is made up of two simple rectangles. No increasing or decreasing is necessary, and the stitch is a simple V stitch. It's a great project for beginners.

Teen Girls' Sizes
One size fits girls' sizes 10, 12, or 14.

Materials
4 skeins (1²/₅ oz or 40 g each) Scot by Unger, or any fluffy yarn to give gauge

teen girl's
fluffy vest

Hooks
Size 6 or G
Size 10½ or K

Gauge
1 pattern sequence = 1 inch (2.5 cm)

Left Side

With larger hook, chain 73 loosely to measure 26 inches (65 cm).
Foundation row: Make 1 double crochet, chain 1, 1 double crochet in 4th chain from hook [1 V stitch made], *skip 2 chains and make 1 V stitch in next stitch, repeat from * ending skip 2 chains, make 1 double crochet in last stitch.
Row 1: Chain 3 to turn, *make 1 V stitch in chain-1 space of V stitch from row below, repeat from * across row, ending with 1 double crochet in top of turning chain. Repeat row 1 till piece measures 9 inches (23.8 cm), end off.

Right Side

Work same as for left side.

Finishing

Holding both rectangles together so that V stitches are going in opposite directions, sew the 2 pieces together along long side halfway up, to form the back. Fold flaps down to form front. Now sew outside edges together 4 inches (10 cm) up from bottom, thereby forming armholes. Work 1 row single crochet around armholes.

To make bottom border and tie: Using smaller hook, chain 40. Attach this chain at bottom left corner of vest, right side facing you, and work single crochet along bottom of vest. When you reach the other side, chain 40. Chain 1 and turn. Working on the stitches added plus the bottom of vest all at one time, work in single crochet for 1 inch (2.5 cm), end off.

Do not block.

modern granny afghan

Here is a new twist on an old favorite—the granny afghan. The center consists of three smaller granny squares sewn together to form a rectangle. Then the yarn is joined and worked round and round to form a giant elongated granny. The great fluffy variegated yarn adds to its charm.

Size
Approximately 60 by 72 inches (152 by 183 cm)

Materials
18 skeins (1¾ oz or 50 g each) Dji Dji by Stanley Berroco, or any brushed wool to give gauge

Hook   **Gauge**
Size P   1 cluster = 2 inches (5 cm)

Note: Yarn is used double strand throughout.

Center Square *(make 3)*
Chain 4, join with slip stitch to form a circle.
Foundation row: Chain 4 [counts as 1 double crochet], work 1 double

crochet, chain 1 11 times in center of circle, join with slip stitch to 3rd stitch of starting chain-4.

Row 1: Chain 3 [counts as 1 double crochet], make 2 more double crochets in same space [this counts as one-half of a corner], *chain 2, skip 3 double crochets, make 3 double crochets, chain 3, make 3 double crochets all in next space [full corner]. Repeat from * twice, chain 2, skip 3 double crochets, make 3 double crochets in same space as you started, chain 2, and join with a slip stitch to top of starting chain 3 [this completes the final corner].

Row 2: Chain 3 [counts as 1 double crochet], make 2 more double crochets in same space [this counts as one-half of a corner], *chain 2, skip 3 double crochets, make 3 double crochets in next space, chain 2, make 3 double crochets, chain 2, make 3 double crochets all in next space [full corner]. Repeat from * twice, chain 2, skip 3 double crochets, make 3 double crochets in next space, chain 2, make 3 double crochets in same space as you started, chain 2, join with slip stitch to top of starting chain 3 [this completes the final corner].

Sew 3 center squares together to form a rectangle. Join yarn in any corner space, chain 3, make 2 more double crochets in same space [this is one-half of corner], *chain 2, skip 3 double crochets, make 3 double crochets in next chain-2 space, repeat from * to next corner, make 3 double crochets, chain 2, make 3 double crochets all in corner space [this is full corner]. Continue work in this manner, keeping corners as established and always having 1 more group of 3 double crochets between each corner after each row, until you have worked 20 rows in all, end off.

Finishing

Starting in any corner, join yarn in chain-2 space. Chain 3, make 5 double crochets in same space, *make 1 single crochet in next chain-2 space, make 5 double crochets in next chain-2 space, repeat from * around entire outside edge of afghan. Join with slip stitch in same space that you started, end off. Do not block.

Girls' Sizes

Directions are for size 8. Changes for sizes 10 and 12 are in parentheses.

Materials

4 (5, 6) skeins (3 oz or 85 g each) of Red Heart Tweedy by Coats & Clark, or any 4-ply yarn to give gauge

Hooks
Size 10½ or K
Size N

Gauge
2 stitches = 1 inch (2.5 cm)

Note: Yarn is used double strand throughout.

Pattern

Row 1: Chain 1 to turn, skip first stitch, *make 1 double crochet in next stitch, 1 single crochet in next stitch, repeat from * across, ending with 1 double crochet in top of turning chain.

   Repeat this row for pattern, being sure that the single crochet is over the double crochet and the double crochet is over the single crochet on all rows.

Back

With smaller hook, chain 8 (8, 9).
Foundation row: Work 1 single crochet from back loop in 2nd chain from hook and 1 single crochet from back loop in each chain to end of row [7, (7, 8) single crochets].
Row 1: Chain 1, turn, skip first stitch [chain-1 counts as first stitch], make 1 single crochet from back loop in each stitch to end of row.

The beautiful texture in this jacket is created by a simple stitch that is a combination single and double crochet. The tweedy yarn used double strand adds lively color.

23

Repeat row 1 for 26 (28, 30) rows. Do not break yarn. Working along long end of band just worked and using larger hook, pick up 1 single crochet in each row [26 (28, 30) single crochets]. Work in pattern stitch till 10½ (11, 11½) inches (25.3, 27.5, 28.8 cm) from beginning. Slip stitch over 2 stitches, work to within 2 stitches of other side (do not work the last 2 stitches). Decrease 1 stitch each side, every other row, 2 times. Work even till armhole is 6½, (6½, 7) inches (16.3, 16.3, 17.5 cm), end off.

Left Front

Work foundation row same as for back. Work band for 13 (14, 15) rows. Change to larger needle and pick up 14 (14, 16) stitches along long end of band. Work in pattern stitch till same length as back to armhole. Shape arm side same as for back. Keep front edge even till 4½ (4½, 5) inches (11.3, 11.3, 12.5 cm) above armhole.

Shape neck as follows: At front edge, slip stitch over 2 stitches, then decrease 1 stitch at neck edge, every row, 2 times. Work even on remaining 6 (6, 8) stitches till shoulder, end off.

Right Front

Work same as for left front, reversing all shaping.

Sleeves

With smaller hook, chain 8 (8, 9). Work foundation row and row 1 same as for back. Repeat row 1 for 16 (18, 20) rows. Do not break yarn. Using larger hook and working along the long end of band, pick up 16 (18, 20) single crochets. Work in pattern stitch till 12 (13, 14) inches (30, 32.5, 35 cm), or desired length to underarm. Slip stitch over 2 stitches, work to within 2 stitches of other side, then, continuing in pattern, decrease 1 stitch each side, every other row, 2 times. Work even till cap of sleeve is 5½ (5½, 6) inches (13.8, 13.8, 15 cm). Work 2 rows even. On next row, change to smaller hook and work 2 stitches together all across row, end off.

Collar

Using smaller hook, chain 13. Work foundation row and row 1 same as for back. Repeat row 1 for 46 (48, 50) rows, end off.

Finishing

Sew shoulder seams, sew underarm seams, and set in sleeves.

Work front border as follows: Using smaller hook, starting at bottom right front, and with right side facing you:

Row 1: Work in single crochet along right front edge to neckline, chain 1, and turn.

Row 2: Work in single crochet, making 5 buttonholes evenly spaced [*to make buttonholes:* chain 2, skip 1 stitch]. Chain 1, turn.

Row 3: Work in single crochet, making 1 single crochet in the buttonhole space.

Work 3 single crochets along left front, starting at neckline and omitting buttonholes. Sew collar in place, pinning at center back and having each front edge about ½ inch (1.25 cm) from edge. Sew collar with right side of collar to wrong side of sweater. Do not block.

woman's cotton pullover

Three strands of cotton yarn and a textured stitch creates the unusual look of this little top. It is a bit more difficult to work with cotton than it is to work with wool yarns, but it is a nice change of pace.

Women's Sizes
Directions are for small size. Changes for medium and large sizes are in parentheses.

Materials
25 (26, 27) skeins Parisian Cotton by Galler, or any cotton yarn to give gauge

Hooks
Size 8 or H
Size 10½ or K

Gauge
2½ stitches = 1 inch (2.5 cm)

Note: Yarn is used triple strand throughout.

Pattern
Row 1: Chain 1 [counts as 1 single crochet], skip first stitch, * make 1 double crochet in next stitch, 1 single crochet in next stitch, repeat from * across row, ending 1 double crochet in top of turning chain.

Repeat this row for pattern, being sure that the single crochet always comes over the double crochet and the double crochet always comes over the single crochet.

25

Back

With smaller hook, chain 11.

Foundation row: Make 1 single crochet in back loop of 2nd chain from hook, 1 single crochet from back loop of each stitch to end of row.

Row 1: Chain 1, turn, skip first stitch, make 1 single crochet from back loop of each stitch to end of row.

Repeat row 1 till 43 (45, 47) rows. Do not break yarn. Change to larger hook, and, working along long edge of band just worked, pick up 44 (46, 48) stitches. Work in pattern stitch till 13 (13½, 14) inches (32.5, 33.8, 35 cm) from beginning, or desired length to underarm. Slip stitch over 3 stitches, work to within 3 stitches of other side, chain, and turn. Being sure to keep pattern as established, decrease 1 stitch each side, every row, 2 times. Work even till armhole is 7 (7½, 8) inches (17.5, 18.8, 20 cm), end off.

Front

Work same as for back to armhole. Shape armhole same as for back,

When last armhole decrease is completed, *shape neck as follows:* Work across 16 (17, 18) stitches, chain 1, and turn. Working on these stitches only, work in pattern till 5 (5½, 6) inches (12.5, 13.8, 15 cm), ending at neck edge. Slip stitch over 6 stitches, work to end of row. Decrease 1 stitch at neck edge, every row, 2 times. Work even on remaining 8 (9, 10) stitches to shoulder, end off.

Skipping 2 stitches in center, join yarn in 3rd stitch from where you divided, and work other side to correspond, reversing all shaping.

Sleeves

Using smaller hook, chain 6. Work foundation row and row 1 same as for back. Repeat row 1 30 (32, 34) times, do not break yarn. Change to larger hook and pick up 30 (32, 34) stitches along long end of band just worked. Working in pattern stitch, work for 3 (3½, 4) inches (7.5, 9, 10 cm). Slip stitch over 3 stitches, work to within 3 stitches of other side, chain, and turn. Being sure to keep pattern as established, decrease 1 stitch each side, every other row, 8 (8, 9) times, end off.

Finishing

Sew shoulders, sew underarm seams, and set in sleeves. With smaller needle, starting at bottom right of front opening, work 3 rows single crochet around front and neck opening as follows:

Row 1: Work single crochets along front edge to neckline, make 3 single crochets in the corner to turn, continue single crocheting around neck opening to other side, make 3 single crochets in the corner to turn, continue down left front.

Row 2: Chain 1, turn, work single crochet over stitches just worked, making 3 single crochets in each corner stitch.

Row 3: Chain 1 and turn, work single crochet over stitches just worked, making 3 single crochets in each corner stitch to turn, end off.

Stitch down ends of crochet, overlapping right over left.

Do not block.

26

Size

Approximately 17 by 11 inches (42.5 by 27.5 cm)

Materials

7 spools (100 yds or 92 m each) Ribbon by Gemini, or any ribbon yarn to give gauge—2 spools each in Colors A and B, 4 spools in Color C

Hook

Size 10 or J

Gauge

2½ stitches = 1 inch (2.5 cm)

Note: 7 spools of ribbon is enough to make 4 placemats.

Body of Placemat

Foundation row: With Color C, chain 35. Make 1 single crochet in 2nd chain from hook, 1 single crochet in each stitch to end of row.
Row 1: Chain 1 to turn, skip first stitch [chain-1 counts as first single crochet], make 1 single crochet in each stitch across row, ending with 1 single crochet in top of turning chain.

Repeat row 1 till piece measures 9 inches (22.5 cm) from the beginning, end off.

Join Color B in same stitch that you ended off, work single crochet along this row. Make 3 single crochets in last stitch, then continue single crocheting along side of piece, picking up 1 single crochet in each row. Make 3 single crochets in last stitch at bottom, continue single crocheting along other side. Make 3 single crochets in last stitch, continue single crocheting along other side to correspond. Make 3 single crochets in last stitch, join with slip stitch to beginning stitch.

Repeat last row once more with Color B, then twice with Color A, end off.

Finishing

Weave in all ends. Do not block. If your placemats look like they should be pressed, "iron" them by placing them under some magazines or heavy books overnight.

ribbon placemats

Festive placemats will brighten up any table setting. These are done in a very simple single crochet stitch with a particularly interesting ribbon yarn to give the great texture.

teen boy's multistriped pullover

Teen Boys' Sizes
Directions are for size 16. Changes for size 18 and 20 are in parentheses.

Materials
10 (11, 12) skeins (1¾ oz or 50 g each) Disco by Unger, or any nubby textured yarn to give gauge
5 skeins (1¾ oz or 50 g each) Petrouchka by Chat Botté—3 skeins in Color A, 2 skeins in Color B—or any worsted weight to give gauge

Hooks
Size 9 or I
Size 10½ or K

Gauge
3 stitches = 1 inch (2.5 cm)

Note: The nubby yarn is used single strand throughout; the worsted yarn is used double strand throughout.

Patterns
Borders: Single crochet from back loop.
Body: Single crochet from both loops in striping pattern as follows:
Rows 1–6: Work in Main Color.
Rows 7 and 8: Work in Color A.
Rows 9 and 10: Work in Color B.

Here a classic pullover is made more interesting through the use of a very nubby yarn combined with two other colors. The contrasting colors pick up the colors of the flecks in the nubby yarn.

Back

With smaller hook and Color A, chain 8.

Foundation row: Work 1 single crochet in 2nd chain from hook, 1 single crochet in each stitch across row [7 stitches].

Row 1: chain 1 to turn, skip first stitch [chain-1 counts as first stitch], make 1 single crochet from back loop in next stitch, make 1 single crochet from back loop in each stitch to end of row.

Repeat row 1 till 48 (51, 54) rows have been worked, do not break yarn. Working along long end of border just worked, pick up 1 stitch in each row [48 (51, 54) single crochets]. Break Color A, join Main Color, and change to larger hook. Work in striping pattern till back is 13 (13½, 14) inches (32.5, 33.8, 35 cm), or desired length to underarm. Continue as established. Slip stitch over 3 stitches, work to within 3 stitches of other side, chain 1, and turn. Decrease 1 stitch each side, every row, 3 times. Work even till armhole is 7 (7½, 8) inches (17.5, 18.8, 20 cm), end off.

Front

Work same as for back till armhole is 5 (5½, 6) inches (12.5, 13.8, 15 cm). Work across 12 (13, 14) stitches, chain 1, and turn. Working on these stitches only and continuing in striping pattern, decrease 1 stitch at neck edge, every row, 2 times. Work even on remaining 10 (11, 12) stitches till armhole is same as back, end off. Skip center 12 (13, 14) stitches. Joining yarn at neck edge, work remaining 12 (13, 14) stitches to correspond.

Sleeves

With Color A and smaller hook, chain 8. Work foundation row and row 1 same as for back till 32 (34, 36) rows have been worked, do not break Color A. Working along long end of border, pick up 1 single crochet in each row [32 (34, 36) single crochets]. Break Color A, join Main Color. Working in striping pattern, increase 1 stitch each side, every 2 inches, 5 times. Continuing as established, work even till sleeve is approximately 15 (15½, 16) inches (38.8, 40, 41.3 cm). [It is very important that you begin the underarm shaping on sleeve with same striping row that you started underarm shaping on back and front. Otherwise stripes will not line up nicely when garment is sewn.] Slip stitch over 3 stitches. Work to within 3 stitches of other side, chain, and turn. Decrease 1 stitch each side, every other row, 10 times. Work even, if necessary, so that top of sleeve matches stripe of body. End off.

Neckband

With Color A and smaller hook, chain 6. Work foundation row and row 1 same as for back for 19 (19½, 20) inches (47.5, 49, 50.3 cm) when slightly stretched. End off.

Finishing

Sew shoulder seams, sew underarm and side seams. Set in sleeves, matching stripes and easing in, rounding shoulder line as you sew. Center neckband around neck opening and stitch in place.

Do not block.

toddler's snowman pullover

Directions are for size 2. Changes for sizes 3 and 4 are in parentheses.

Materials
4 (4, 5) skeins (1¾ oz or 50 g each) Domani by Angora Corporation of America, or any baby yarn to give gauge
1 skein (⅓ oz or 10 g each) white Angora by Angora Corporation of America, or any angora to give gauge
small amount of black fingering yarn for trim
3 buttons

Hook
Size 10 or J

Gauge
3 stitches = 1 inch (2.5 cm)

Note: Baby yarn is used double strand throughout; angora is used single strand.

Back
Chain 8.
Foundation row: Make 1 single crochet in 2nd chain from hook, 1 single crochet in each chain to end of row [7 (7, 7) single crochets].
Row 1: Chain 1, turn, skip first stitch [chain-1 counts as first stitch], make 1 single crochet from back loop in next stitch, 1 single crochet from back loop in each stitch to end of row.

Repeat row 1 till you have worked 34 (36, 38) rows. Working along long end of border just worked, pick up 1 single crochet in each row [34 (36, 38) single crochets]. Continue working in single crochet from both loops till 8 (8½, 9) inches (20, 21.3, 22.5 cm), or desired length to underarm. Slip stitch over 2 stitches, work to within 2 stitches of other side, chain 1, and turn. Work even on 30 (32, 34) stitches, till armhole is 4½ (5, 5½) inches (11.3, 12.5, 13.8 cm), end off.

Front
Work same as for back till armhole is 3 (3½, 4) inches (7.5, 8.8, 10 cm).
Shape neck as follows: Work across 10 (11, 12) stitches, chain 1, and turn. Working on these stitches only, decrease 1 stitch at neck edge, every row, 2 times. Work even on remaining 8 (9, 10) stitches till same as back to shoulder, end off. Skip center 10 stitches and work remaining 10 (11, 12) stitches to correspond.

Sleeves
Chain 8. Work foundation row and row 1 same as for back. Continue to repeat row 1 till 20 (22, 24) rows have been worked. Working along long end of border just worked, pick up 1 single crochet in each row. Next row, working in single crochet from both loops, increase 1 stitch at beginning and end of row [22 (24, 26) single crochets in all]. Continue to work in pattern as established, increasing 1 stitch each side every 1½ inches (3.8 cm), 3 times [28, (30, 32) stitches]. Work even till sleeve is 8½ (9, 9½) inches (21.3, 22.5, 23.8 cm). Slip stitch over 2 stitches, work to within 2 stitches of other side, chain 1, and

turn. Continue as established, decreasing 1 stitch each side, every other row, 5 (5, 6) times, end off.

Snowman

With angora yarn, chain 15. Work in single crochet from the whole stitch for 12 rows, then decrease 1 stitch each side, every row, 5 times [4 stitches remain]. Increase 1 stitch each side, every row, 2 times [8 stitches]. Work even for 4 rows, then decrease 1 stitch each side, every row, 2 times, end off.

Snowman's Scarf

With single strand of fingering yarn, chain 45. Work single crochet for 4 rows, end off. Fringe ends (see page 7).

Snowman's Hat

With small amount of black fingering yarn, chain 9. Work single crochet for 2 rows, end off. Working on center 4 stitches only, work single crochet for 4 rows, end off.

Finishing

Sew right shoulder. Sew left shoulder ½ inch (1.3 cm) in from outside edge. Set in sleeves, sew underarm seams. Starting at right shoulder, work 1 row single crochet all around neckline, work 1 row backward single crochet to end of front neck shaping. Work 3 buttonloops on left front shoulder [*to make buttonloops:* chain 3, skip 1 stitch]. Sew on buttons.

Sew snowman's scarf around snowman's neck. Then sew snowman to front of sweater. Sew hat in place. Using black fingering yarn, embroider eyes and nose. Using angora yarn, embroider snowflakes all around front, using either duplicate stitch embroidery or French knots.

Do not block.

His or her very own snowman in a shower of snowflakes is sure to delight a toddler. Side buttons at the shoulder make for easy on-and-off.

31

girl's striped pullover

Girls' Sizes
Directions are for size 8. Changes for sizes 10 and 12 are in parentheses.

Materials
8 (9, 10) skeins (1¾ oz or 50 g each) Spectrum by Unger, or any bulky tweed yarn to give gauge
1 (1, 2) skein(s) (1¾ oz or 50 g each) Dji Dji by Stanley Berroco, or any brushed wool to give gauge

Hook   Gauge
Size N   2 stitches = 1 inch (2.5 cm)

Note: Bulky yarn is used single strand; brushed wool is used double strand throughout.

Striping Pattern
Rows 1–6: With bulky yarn, work single crochet.
Rows 7 and 8: With brushed wool, work single crochet.
   Repeat these 8 rows.

Back
With bulky yarn, chain 29 (31, 33).
Foundation row: Work 1 single crochet in 2nd chain from hook, make 1 single crochet in each chain thereafter [28 (30, 32) single crochets].
Row 1: Chain 1 to turn, skip first stitch [chain-1 counts as first stitch], make 1 single crochet in each stitch to end of row.
   Repeat row 1, working in striping pattern, till back measures 9 (10, 11) inches (22.5, 25, 27.5 cm), or desired length to armhole. Slip stitch over first 2 stitches, work single crochet to within 2 stitches of end of row. Do not work last 2 stitches, chain 1, and turn. Continuing in pattern as established, decrease 1 stitch each side, every other row, 2 times. Work even till armhole measures 6 (6½, 7) inches (15, 16.3, 17.5 cm), end off.

Front
Work same as for back till armhole is 4 (4½, 5) inches (10, 11.3, 12.5 cm).
   Shape neck as follows: Work single crochet across next 8 (9, 9) stitches, chain 1, and turn. Working on these stitches only, decrease 1 stitch at neck edge, every row, 3 times [5 (6, 6) stitches left]. Work on these last 5 (6, 6) stitches, till armhole is same as back, end off. Skipping the center 4 (4, 6) stitches, join yarn at neck edge and complete other side to correspond.

Sleeves
With bulky yarn, chain 17 (19, 21). Work in single crochet same as for back, increasing 1 stitch each side, every 3 (3½, 4) inches (7.5, 9, 10 cm), 3 times. Work even till 12 (12½, 13) inches (30, 31.3, 32.5 cm). Slip stitch over 2 stitches, work to within 2 stitches of other side, chain 1, turn. Continuing in pattern, decrease 1 stitch each side, every row, 2 times. Work even till cap of sleeve measures 6 (6½, 7) inches (15, 16.3, 17.5 cm). Next row, work 2 stitches together all across row, end off.

Finishing

Sew all seams, being sure to match stripes on back and front.

Using brushed wool, double strand, *work picot edging around neckline, bottom of sleeves, and bottom of pullover as follows:* With right side facing you, starting at a seam, work 1 row single crochet all around opening, join with a slip stitch. Chain 3, make 1 single crochet in same stitch that chain-3 is coming from, skip 1 stitch, make 1 single crochet in next stitch, *chain 3, make 1 single crochet in same stitch, skip 1 stitch, make 1 single crochet in next stitch. Repeat from * around, ending with a slip stitch, end off.

If blocking is needed, wet in cool water, lay flat to dry. Do not steam.

Girls love pretty sweaters that can be worn casually over just about anything they own. This soft pullover with bright contrasting stripes, done in a puffy variegated yarn, is fun to make and fun to wear. Crocheted in a very simple stitch, it is the yarn itself that makes this sweater interesting. Picot edges add a slightly feminine touch.

33

The highly textured bulky yarn, the easy fit of the dropped shoulder, combined with an easy stitch done on a large hook, make this jacket a sure winner.

34

Women's Sizes

Directions are for small size. Changes for medium and large sizes are in parentheses.

Materials

3 skeins (3½ oz or 100 g each) Aspen Bulky Yarn by Brunswick, or any bulky yarn to give gauge
7 (8, 9) skeins (2 oz or 60 g each) of Millefiore by Stanley Berocco, or any textured yarn to give gauge
7 large buttons

Hooks   Gauge

Size 10 or J   2 stitches = 1 inch (2.5 cm)
Size N

Note: The bulky yarn is used single strand; the textured yarn is used double strand throughout.

Back

Starting at waistband, with bulky yarn and smaller hook, chain 10.
Foundation row: Starting in 2nd chain from hook, make 1 single crochet in next stitch, make 1 single crochet in each stitch to end of row [9 single crochets].
Row 1: Chain 1 to turn, skip first stitch, make 1 single crochet from back loop in next stitch, make 1 single crochet from back loop in each stitch to end of row, make 1 stitch in top of turning chain.

Continue to repeat row 1 till waistband has 36 (38, 40) rows worked [each ridge is 2 rows], end off. Join textured yarn, and using larger hook, pick up 36 (38, 40) single crochets along long end of waistband, picking up 1 stitch in each row [36 (38, 40) single crochets]. Chain 1, turn, skip first stitch [chain-1 counts as first stitch], make 1 single crochet in each stitch across row, make 1 single crochet in top of turning chain.

Continue to repeat the last row till piece is 14 (14½, 15) inches (35, 36.3, 37.5 cm) from beginning. Slip stitch over 2 stitches, work to within 2 stitches of other side, chain 1, turn. Continue to work single crochet on the remaining 32 (34, 36) stitches till armhole is 7 (7½, 8) inches, end off.

Left Front

Start waistband same as for back. Work for 18 (19, 20) rows, end off. Join textured yarn and pick up 18 (19, 20) stitches along long end of waistband. Using larger hook, continue single crochet till same as back to armhole. Slip stitch over 2 stitches, work to end of row. Continue to single crochet on the remaining 16 (17, 18) stitches till armhole is 5 (5½, 6) inches (12.5, 13.8, 15 cm), ending at neck edge.

Shape neck as follows: Slip stitch over 4 stitches, work single crochet to end of row. Chain 1, turn, work single crochet, decreasing 1 stitch at neck edge every row, 4 times. Work even on remaining 8 (9, 10) stitches until armhole is 7 (7½, 8) inches (17.5, 18.8, 20 cm), end off.

Right Front

Work same as for left front, reversing all shaping.

woman's
dropped-
shoulder
jacket

Sleeves

Start cuff, same as for back waistband. Work single crochet through back loop for 20 (22, 24) rows. Using larger hook, join textured yarn and pick up 20 (22, 24) stitches along long side of cuff. Continue in single crochet pattern, increasing 1 stitch each side, every 2½ inches (6 cm), 4 times. Continue on the 28 (30, 32) stitches until sleeve is 17½ (18, 18½) inches (42.5, 43.8, 45 cm) from beginning. End off textured yarn. Still using larger hook, join bulky yarn. Next row, increase 6 (7, 8) stitches evenly across row. Continue on the 35 (37, 40) stitches in single crochet from back loop for 2 inches (5 cm), end off.

Collar

With smaller hook and bulky yarn, chain 15 (15, 15). Work foundation row and pattern same as for back waistband for 38 (40, 42) rows, end off.

Finishing

Sew the 8 (9, 10) stitches of shoulder seams together.

To set in sleeves: Fold each sleeve in half, marking center. Pin in sleeve, matching center point with shoulder seam and having ends of sleeve meet bound-off stitches of back and front at armhole. Sew sleeve only after pinning and checking that all is centered. Sew underarm seams.

To set in collar: Find center point of collar and center point of back. Pin collar in place, having each end of collar reach right to the end of each front. Stitch 1 side of collar to sweater body. Then fold collar in half to inside and stitch in place.

To make front border: Starting at bottom right front, with bulky yarn and smaller hook, work single crochet along right front, working through both thicknesses of collar. Chain 1, turn. Work a 2nd row of single crochet, making 7 buttonholes evenly spaced [*to make buttonholes:* chain 2, skip 1 stitch], having first buttonhole start about 3 stitches from top and last buttonhole about same distance from bottom. Chain 1, turn. Make a 3rd row of single crochet, making 1 single crochet in chain-2 space of each buttonhole, end off. Work 3 rows of single crochet on left front in same manner, starting at collar and being sure that you pick up the same amount of stitches that were picked up for right front. Omit buttonholes on left front.

Do not block.

Men's Sizes

Directions are for size 36–38. Changes for sizes 40–42 and 44–46 are in parentheses.

man's reversible vest

Men will love the sporty look of this reversible vest. Made in simple single crochet, one side is a very heavily textured curly yarn, one side is a smooth wool.

Materials

9 (9, 10) skeins (1¾ oz or 50 g each) Dorothy by Fantacia, or any curly yarn to give gauge
5 (5, 6) skeins (1¾ oz or 50 g each) Allora by Fantacia, or any bulky yarn to give gauge
10 leather buttons

Hooks   Gauge

Size 10 or J   2 stitches = 1 inch (2.5 cm) on smaller hook
Size 10½ or K   2½ stitches = 1 inch (2.5 cm) on larger hook

Note: It is very important that lining pieces match vest pieces exactly.

Back (textured side)

With larger hook and curly yarn, chain 45 (47, 49).
Foundation row: Work 1 single crochet in 2nd chain from hook, 1 single crochet in each stitch across row.
Row 1: Chain 1, turn, skip first stitch [chain-1 counts as first stitch], work 1 single crochet in each stitch to end of row.

Repeat row 1 till 10 (10½, 11) inches (25, 26.6, 27.3 cm) from beginning. Slip stich over 3 stitches, work to within 3 stitches of other side, chain, and turn. Continuing in single crochet, decrease 1 stitch each side, every row, 3 times. Work even on remaining 32 (34, 36) stitches until armhole is 10 (10½, 11) inches (25, 25.3, 27.5 cm), end off.

Left Front

Chain 25 (26, 27). Work same as for back, till armhole, ending at arm side. Slip stitch over 3 stitches, then decrease 1 stitch at arm side, every row, 3 times. Continue on remaining 18 (19, 20) stitches until armhole is 8 (8½, 9) inches (20, 21.3, 22.5 cm), ending at neck edge. Slip stitch over 6 stitches, then decrease 1 stitch at neck edge, every row, 5 times. Work even on remaining 7 (8, 9) stitches till armhole is same as back, end off.

Right Front

Work same as for left front, reversing all shaping. Sew shoulder seams and underarm seams and set aside.

Back (smooth side)

With smaller hook and bulky yarn, chain 55 (57, 60). Work same as for back (textured side), until armhole. Slip stitch over 4 stitches, work to within 4 stitches other side, chain, and turn. Decrease 1 stitch each side, every row, 4 times. Work even on remaining 46 (48, 51) stitches till armhole is 10 (10½, 11) inches (25, 25.3, 27.5 cm), end off.

Left Front

With smaller hook and bulky yarn, chain 30 (32, 33). Work same as for back till armhole, ending at arm side. Slip stitch over 4 stitches, then decrease 1 stitch arm side only, every row, 4 times. Continue on remaining 21 (23, 24) stitches till armhole is 8 (8½, 9) inches (20, 21.3,

22.5 cm), ending at neck edge. Slip stitch over 7 stitches, then decrease 1 stitch neck edge, every row, 5 (6, 6) times. Continue on remaining 9 (10, 11) stitches till same as back, end off. Sew shoulder and side seams.

Finishing

Pin both textured and smooth vest together, with wrong sides facing each other. Pin all around edges and armholes, being sure that seams match. With larger hook and curly yarn, working through both thicknesses, join yarn at bottom right underarm seam and *work border as follows:*

Row 1: Work single crochet along bottom to right front, make 3 single crochets in corner to turn, continue single crocheting up right front, make 3 single crochets in corner to turn. Continue single crocheting around neckline, pulling in slightly. Make 3 single crochets in corner to turn, continue down left front, make 3 single crochets in corner to turn, continue along bottom back to where you started, join with a slip stitch to first single crochet, do not turn.

Row 2: Repeat row 1, making 5 evenly spaced buttonholes on left front [*to make buttonholes:* chain 2, skip 1 stitch].

Row 3: Repeat row 1, making 1 single crochet in each chain-2 space of buttonhole. End off.

Sew buttons. Do not block.

woman's pierrot-collar jacket

Women's Sizes

Directions are for small size. Changes for medium and large sizes are in parentheses.

Materials

8 (9, 10) skeins (3½ oz or 100 g each) Aspen Bulky Yarn by Brunswick, or any bulky yarn to give gauge
6 (7, 8) skeins (2 oz or 60 g each) of Millefiore by Stanley Berocco, or any textured yarn to give gauge
7 large buttons

Hooks

10½ or K
Size N

Gauge

2 stitches = 1 inch (2.5 cm)

Note: The bulky yarn is used single strand; the textured yarn is used double strand throughout.

Back

Starting at waistband, with smaller hook and bulky yarn, chain 37 (39, 41)
Foundation row: Starting in 2nd chain from hook, make 1 single crochet from back loop, make 1 single crochet from back loop in each stitch to end of row [36 (38, 40) single crochets from back loop].
Row 1: Chain 1 to turn, skip first stitch [chain-1 counts as first stitch], make 1 single crochet from back loop in each stitch to end, make 1 single crochet in top of turning chain.

Continue to repeat Row 1 till waistband is 2½ (2½, 3) inches (6, 6, 7.5 cm).
Next row: With larger hook, chain 1 to turn, work single crochet through both loops in first stitch [this is an increase, as the first stitch is usually skipped]. Work single crochet through both loops in each stitch across row, make 2 single crochets in last stitch [2nd increase]. You now have 38 (40, 42) single crochet on back.

Continue to single crochet through both loops, till piece measures 11 ½ (12, 12½) inches (28.8, 30, 31.3 cm) from beginning. Slip stitch over 2 stitches, work to within 2 stitches other side, chain 1, turn. Continue in single crochet pattern, decreasing 1 stitch each side, every row, 2 times [30 (32, 34) stitches]. Do not break bulky yarn. Join textured yarn. Start striping pattern: carrying yarn up as you work and continuing in single crochet pattern, alternate working 2 rows of textured yarn and 2 rows of bulky yarn, until armhole is 7 (7½, 8) inches (17.5, 18.8, 20 cm), end off.

Left Front

With smaller hook and bulky yarn, chain 19 (20, 21). Work foundation row and pattern same as for back to armhole. At arm side, slip stitch over 2 stitches, work to end of row. Chain 1, turn. Continue to single crochet, decreasing 1 stitch at arm side only, every row, 2 times, [14 (15, 16) stitches left]. Do not break bulky yarn, join textured yarn and work

This is truly an unusual jacket, with its feminine, ruffled collar, interesting striped yoke, and contrasting sleeves. Pair it with a matching skirt for a great suit look.

41

striping pattern same as for back till armhole is 5 (5½, 6) inches (12.5, 13.8, 15 cm), ending at neck edge. Being sure to keep striping pattern as established, slip stitch over 4 stitches, continue to end of row. Then decrease 1 stitch at neck edge, every row, 3 times. Work in pattern on remaining 7 (8, 9) stitches until armhole is 7 (7½, 8) inches (17.5, 18.8, 20 cm), end off.

Right Front
Work same as for left front, reversing all shaping.

Sleeves
With smaller hook and bulky yarn, chain 28 (30, 32). Work same as for back for border, break off bulky yarn.

With larger hook and textured yarn, increase 1 stitch at beginning and end of next row [29, 31, 33 stitches]. Continue in single crochet, through both loops, till sleeve is 16 (16, 16½) inches (40, 40, 41.3 cm), or desired length to underarm. Slip stitch over 2 stitches, work to within 2 stitches of other side, chain 1, and turn. Continuing in pattern as established, decrease 1 stitch each side, every row, twice. Work even on remaining stitches till cap of sleeve measures 7 (7½, 8) inches (17.5, 18.8, 20 cm). On next row, work 2 stitches together all across row, end off.

Finishing
Sew the 7 (8, 9) stitches of shoulders together. Set in sleeves, sew underarm seams.

To make front border: With textured yarn and smaller hook, starting at top left edge, work 3 rows of single crochet along left front, end off. Before starting right front border, mark 7 evenly spaced buttonholes using left border as your guide. Starting at bottom right corner, work 1 row single crochet on right front, chain 1, turn. Work a 2nd row, making 7 evenly spaced buttonholes on this row [*to make buttonholes:* chain 2, skip 1 stitch], chain 1, turn. Work a 3rd row of single crochet, making 1 single crochet in the chain-2 space of each buttonhole, end off.

Make Pierrot collar as follows:

Foundation row: Using smaller hook and textured yarn, work 1 row single crochet all around neckline.

Row 1: Chain 8, turn, *work 1 single crochet from back loop of next stitch, chain 8, repeat from * to end of row. *Continuing along other side of the foundation row stitches,* continue the chain 8 and single crochet in other half of stitch.

Row 2: Chain 8, work 1 single crochet into very first loop made, *chain 8, make 1 single crochet into next loop, repeat from * all around, back to where you started.

Row 3: Repeat row 2, end off.

Sew on buttons. Do not block.

Teen Boys' Sizes

Directions are written for size 14. Changes for size 16 and 18 are in parentheses.

Materials

5 (5, 6) skeins (3½ oz or 100 g each) Brunswick Knitting Worsted, or any other knitting worsted to give gauge in Main Color
3 skeins (1¾ oz or 50 g each) Petrouchka by Chat Botté—1 skein each in Colors A, B, and C—or any knitting worsted to give gauge

Hooks	**Gauge**
Size 8 or G	3 stitches = 1 inch (2.5 cm)
Size 10 or J	

Back

With smaller hook and Main Color, chain 52 (55, 58) loosely.
Foundation row: Work single crochet in 2nd chain from hook, 1 single crochet in each stitch to end of row [51 (54, 57) single crochets].
Row 1: Chain 1, turn, skip first stitch [chain-1 counts as first stitch], make 1 single crochet in each stitch to end of row, make 1 single crochet in top of turning chain.

Repeat row 1, 3 times more. Change to larger hook, and repeat row 1 till 20 (21, 22) inches (51, 52.5, 55 cm) from beginning, end off.

Front

With smaller hook and Main Color, chain 37 (40, 43) loosely. Work foundation row and first 4 rows same as for back. Change to larger hook and continue same as for back till piece measures 18 (19, 20) inches (45, 47.5, 50 cm) from beginning, end off.

Sleeves

With smaller hook and Main Color, chain 30 (33, 36) loosely. Work foundation row and first 4 rows same as for back. Change to larger hook

teen boy's motif pullover

Hard-to-please teenagers will surely love this pullover. Boldly colored motifs on a solid color background make a striking contrast.

43

and work in single crochet pattern, increasing 1 stitch each side, every 2 inches (5 cm), 8 times. Continue in pattern till sleeve measures 18 (18½, 19) inches (45, 45.3, 47.5 cm) from beginning, end off.

Motif (make 5)
Each motif must be 4 inches (10 cm) square.

Foundation row: Using larger hook and Color A, chain 4, join with slip stitch to form ring.

Row 1: Chain 4 [counts as 1 double crochet], make 11 more double crochets in ring, join with a slip stitch to top of chain-4. End off Color A.

Row 2: Join Color B in any space between 2 double crochets, chain 4 [this counts as 1 double crochet], make 2 more double crochets in same space [this is half a corner],* skip 3 double crochets, chain 1, make 3 double crochets in next space, chain 1, make 3 double crochets in same space, repeat from * twice, skip 3 double crochets, chain 1, make 3 double crochets in same space that you began, chain 1, join with slip stitch to top of chain-4 [this completes corner.] End off Color B.

Row 3: Join Color C in any corner space, chain 4, make 2 more double crochets in same space [this is half corner] *chain 1, make 3 double crochets in next chain-1 space, make 3 double crochets, chain 1, 3 double crochets all in next corner space, repeat from * twice, chain 1, make 3 double crochets in next chain-1 space, chain 1, make 3 double crochets in same space that you started in, chain 1, join with slip stitch to top of chain 4. End off Color C.

Row 4: With Main Color, starting in any corner space, make 3 single crochets, chain 1, 3 single crochets, make 1 single crochet in each stitch to next corner, *make 3 single crochets, chain 1, 3 single crochets all in corner space, make 1 single crochet in each stitch to next corner, repeat from * once, end with 1 single crochet in each stitch, back to where you started, join with a slip stitch, end off.

Sew 5 motifs together in a long row to measure 20 inches (50 cm). [for sizes 16 and 18, join Main Color to top of row of motifs, and, working in single crochet, add 1 inch (2.5 cm) for size 16 and 2 inches (5 cm) for size 18, end off.]

Finishing
Sew row of motifs to left side of front, starting at the bottom. This will leave 2 inches (5 cm) overhanging at top of front. Join Main Color 5 inches (12.5 cm) in from other side, and work in single crochet for 2 inches (12.5 cm), end off. The top of the motif row and the 2 inches (5 cm) added at top form neck shaping and shoulders. Sew back and front together at shoulders. Fold sleeves in half and mark center. Pin sleeves in place, centering on shoulder seam and sewing down 7½ (8, 8½) inches (18.8, 20, 21.3 cm) on each side of shoulder seam. Sew under-arm seams.

To make neckband: starting at shoulder, using Main Color and smaller hook, work 5 rows single crochet around neckline, pulling in slightly as you work, end off.

Do not block.

Materials for "Hers"

6 skeins (2 oz or 60 g each) Aspen by Brunswick or any bulky yarn to give gauge

1 oz (28 g) each, any worsted weight yarn in Colors A, B, C, D, for flowers

Materials for "His"

6 skeins (3½ oz or 100 g each) Germantown Knitting Worsted by Brunswick—2 skeins each in Colors A, B, and C—or any yarn to give gauge

1 yard elastic cord

Hooks

Size 6 or G
Size 10½ or K

Gauge

2½ stitches = 1 inch (2.5 cm)

Note: Knitting worsted is used triple strand throughout.

All Covers

Using larger hook, chain 36.

Foundation row: Make 1 single crochet in 2nd chain from hook, 1 single crochet in each chain to end of row [35 single crochets].

Row 1: Chain 1, turn, skip first stitch [chain-1 counts as first stitch], make 1 single crochet from back loop in next stitch, 1 single crochet from back loop in each stitch to end of row.

Repeat row 1 for 22 rows, end off. Fold in half lengthwise, and sew together. Then, using same thread, gather one end, pulling together and anchoring tightly. This is now the top of the golf cover. Turn inside out, sew in elastic cord about 6 inches (15 cm) from the top, gathering slightly.

decorated golf club covers

All the golf covers shown are made with the same instructions. We just added flowers to the basic covers to make very pretty covers for "her." The more classic ones are for "him." We used three different colors, then used them all together for the fourth cover.

45

Covers for Her

Make 4 basic covers with the bulky yarn. Make flowers in a different color for each cover.

Flowers

With smaller hook and worsted yarn, chain 46.

Row 1: Make 1 double crochet in 4th chain from hook, *chain 2, skip 2 chains, 1 double crochet in the next stitch, chain 2, 1 double crochet in the same stitch, repeat from * across row.

Row 2: Chain 4, turn, 1 double crochet in the first space, *chain 2, double crochet in the next space, chain 2, double crochet in the same space, repeat from * across row.

Row 3: Chain 2, 7 double crochets in the next space, *single crochet in next space, 8 double crochets in the next space, repeat from * to end of row, end off.

Thread about 18 inches of yarn onto a tapestry needle and gather along the chain end of flower, pull up tightly, and sew securely. Sew to top of golf club cover.

Covers for Him

Using worsted weight yarn triple strand, following basic instructions, make 1 cover in Color A, 1 cover in Color B, 1 cover in Color C, and 1 cover using 1 strand each of Colors A, B, and C. Make large pom-poms and sew in place.

Pom-Poms

Wind yarn 150 times around a 5-inch (12.5-cm) piece of cardboard. Tie very securely in the center. Cut each end, shake out vigorously, and trim.

girl's ombré striped pullover

Solid stripes, combined with an ombré yarn, add interest to this classic pullover. Add a ruffled neckline and side button closing for a totally feminine look.

Girls' Sizes

Directions are for size 8. Changes for size 10 and 12 are in parentheses.

Materials

5 (6, 7) skeins (2 oz or 60 g each) Print Silky Spun by Melrose, or any bulky yarn to give gauge
4 (4, 5) skeins (2 oz or 60 g each) Solid Silky Spun by Melrose, or any bulky yarn to give gauge
2 buttons

Hooks

Size 10 or J
Size 10½ or K

Gauge

5 stitches = 2 inches (5 cm)

Back

With smaller hook and solid yarn, chain 9.
Foundation row: Make 1 single crochet in 2nd chain from hook, 1 single crochet in each stitch to end of row [8 single crochets].

47

Row 1: Chain 1 to turn, skip first stitch [chain-1 counts as first stitch], make 1 single crochet from back loop in next stitch, make 1 single crochet from back loop in each stitch to end of row.

Repeat row 1 till 36 (38, 40) rows have been worked, do not end off. Working along long edge of border, work 1 single crochet in each row across [36 (38, 40) stitches]. Chain 1, turn, using the larger hook and solid yarn, work single crochet for 5 rows more. Do not break yarn, join print yarn, and continue in single crochet for 4 rows more, do not break yarn. Carrying yarn loosely up sides as you work, continue to work 6 rows of solid and 4 rows of print until 10½ (11, 11½) inches (25.3, 27.5, 28.8 cm), or desired length to underarm. Slip stitch over 2 stitches, work to within 2 stitches of other side. Chain 1, turn. Continuing in pattern as established, decrease 1 stitch each side, every row, 2 times. Still continuing in pattern as established, work even till armhole is 6 (6½, 7) inches (15, 16.3, 17.5 cm), end off.

Front

Work same as for back till armhole is 4½ (5, 5½) inches (11.3, 12.5, 13.8 cm).

Shape neck as follows: Work across 8 (9, 10) stitches, chain 1, turn. Working on these stitches only, decrease 1 stitch neck edge, every row, 2 times. Work even till armhole is same as back. Skipping the center 12 stitches, work 8 (9, 10) stitches of other side to correspond, end off.

Sleeves

Using smaller hook and solid yarn, work foundation row and border same as for back until 18 (20, 22) rows have been worked. Break solid yarn. Using larger hook and print yarn, pick up 1 stitch in each row along long edge of border [18 (20, 22) stitches]. Chain 1, turn. On next row, increase evenly to 26 (38, 30) stitches. Continuing in single crochet and print yarn, work even till sleeve is 11 (11½, 12) inches (27.5, 28.8, 30 cm), or desired length to underarm. Slip stitch over 2 stitches, work to within 2 stitches of other side, chain 1, turn. Work even on remaining 22 (24, 26) stitches till cap of sleeve is 5½ (6, 6½) inches (13.8, 15, 16.3 cm). Next row, work 2 stitches together all across row, end off.

Finishing

Sew right shoulder. Sew left shoulder ½ inch (1.3 cm) in from outside edge. Sew underarm seams, set in sleeves.

Work neck ruffle as follows: Starting at back left shoulder, with print yarn and smaller hook, work single crochet along shoulder to the ½-inch seam, then continue single crocheting on other side of shoulder, making 2 buttonloops on this side [*to make buttonloops:* chain 4, skip 1 stitch]. Continue single crocheting all around neck opening, do not end off. Chain 1 and turn. Working on single crochets of neck opening only, and not on the stitches of shoulder, work as follows: *Chain 8, make 1 single crochet in back loop of next stitch, repeat from * all around. Working in front loop of same stitches, repeat last row, end off. Sew 2 buttons to back side of left shoulder. Do not block.

48

Women's Sizes
Directions are for size 8. Changes for size 10 and 12 are in parentheses.

Materials
10 (11, 12) skeins (1²/₅ oz or 40 g each) Samida Mohair by Melrose, or any mohair to give gauge
2 (2, 3) skeins (⁷/₁₀ oz or 20 g each) Ariane by Unger, or any glitter yarn to give gauge.

Hook
Size 10½ or K

Gauge
5 double crochets = 2 inches (5 cm)

Note: The mohair yarn is used single strand, the glitter yarn, double strand, throughout.

Back
With mohair yarn, chain 45 (48, 51).
Foundation row: Make 1 double crochet in 3rd chain from hook, 1 double crochet in each chain to end of row [42 (45, 48) double crochets].
Row 1: Chain 3 to turn, skip first stitch [chain-3 counts as first double crochet], 1 double crochet in each stitch to end of row, 1 double crochet in top of turning chain, do not break mohair.

woman's mohair and glitter chanel jacket

Just a touch of glitter turns this classic little chanel jacket into a great evening look. Pair it with the Woman's Glitter Camisole (see page 51) for a special occasion.

Row 2: Join glitter yarn, work 1 single crochet in each stitch across row.
Row 3: Chain 1, turn. Repeat row 2.
Rows 4 and 5: Repeat row 1.
Rows 6 and 7: Repeat row 2.
Rows 8 and 9: Repeat row 1.
Rows 10 and 11: Repeat row 2. Break glitter yarn.

Continuing to repeat row 1, work till 10 (10½, 11) inches (25, 25.3, 27.5 cm). Slip stitch over 2 stitches, work to within 2 stitches of other side, chain 1, turn. Continue to repeat row 1 till armhole is 7 (7½, 8) inches (17.5, 18.8, 20 cm), end off.

Left Front

With mohair yarn, chain 26 (27, 28). Work foundation row and striping pattern same as for back, till armhole. At arm side, slip stitch over 2 stitches, work even till armhole is 5 (5½, 6) inches (12.5, 13.8, 15 cm), ending at neck edge. Slip stitch over 8 (9, 10) stitches, then decrease 1 stitch at neck edge, every row, 4 (3, 2) times. Work even on remaining 9 (10, 11) stitches till same as back, end off.

Right Front

Work same as for left front, reversing all shaping.

Sleeves

With mohair yarn, chain 38 (40, 42). Work foundation row and row 1 same as for back. Continue to repeat row 1 of back till sleeve is 10 (10½, 11) inches (25, 25.3, 27.5 cm), then repeat striping pattern as on back, end off.

Tie

With mohair yarn, chain 150. Work foundation row and row 1 same as for back. Repeat row 1, 2 times more, end off.

Finishing

Sew shoulder seams. Sew underarm seams. Fold sleeve in half and mark center. Line up center mark with shoulder seam, and sew sleeve into armhole [this is a dropped shoulder and the sleeve has no cap; the last row of double crochet is sewn into armhole].

To make front border: Starting at bottom right side, with mohair, work 3 rows single crochet along front edge, end off. Starting at top left side, with mohair, work 3 rows single crochet along front edge, end off.

To make ruffle collar: Starting at top right side, work 1 row double crochet along neck, pulling in slightly, do not break yarn. Chain 6, turn, make 1 single crochet in back loop of first double crochet, *chain 6, make 1 single crochet in back loop of next stitch, repeat from * to end of row. Continuing along other side of chain, repeat from * back to where you started from, join with a slip stitch into first stitch, do not break yarn. On next row, *chain 6, make 1 single crochet in next chain-6 loop, repeat from * all around entire collar, join with a slip stitch, end off. Weave tie in and out of double crochet row.

Do not block.

Women's Sizes
Directions are for size 8. Changes for sizes 10 and 12 are in parentheses.

Materials
4 (5, 6) skeins (7/10 oz or 20 g each) Ariane by Unger, or any glitter yarn to give gauge
2 buttons

Hooks
Size 9 or I
Size 10½ or K

Gauge
3 stitches = 1 inch (2.5 cm) on larger hook

Notes: Yarn is used double strand throughout.

Back
With larger hook, chain 49 (52, 55).
Foundation row: With smaller hook, work 1 single crochet in 2nd chain from hook, 1 single crochet in each chain across row.
Row 1: Chain 1 to turn, still using smaller hook, skip the first stitch [chain-1 counts as first stitch], make 1 single crochet in each stitch to end of row.

Repeat row 1 for 2 inches (5 cm). Change to larger hook and continue to repeat row 1 till 10½, (11, 11½) inches (25.3, 27.5, 28.8 cm), from the beginning, or desired length, end off.

Front
Work same as for back.

Finishing
Sew side seams.

Make straps as follows: Starting at side seam, working along top back of camisole, make single crochets till 4 inches in from side seam. Do not break yarn. Using same yarn, make a chain 28 inches (70 cm) long. With hook still in last loop of chain, make a single crochet in same stitch that chain started in (this creates a long double chain that will form strap of camisole). Continue single crochet along top back of camisole until 4 inches (10 cm) from other side, make another strap to correspond. Continuing along top of camisole with single crochet, work back to where you started. Join with slip stitch, end off. Sew strap about ½ inch (1.3 cm) from fold in strap that was created when chain was doubled. This forms a buttonloop. Sew buttons on front of camisole.

Do not block.

What baby wouldn't love to cuddle up in this unusual baby blanket? It is crocheted in bulky yarn, and puff stitches form the diamond pattern. Although not a project for beginners, it is not actually as difficult to make as it looks.

Size
Approximately 26 by 36 inches (65 by 90 cm)

Materials
12 skeins (2 oz or 60 g each) Aspen by Brunswick, or any bulky yarn to give gauge

Hook   Gauge
Size 15   1½ stitches = 1 inch (2.5 cm)

Patterns
Popcorn is worked on 1 stitch as follows: Double crochet 5 times in same stitch, remove hook and insert in front of first double crochet in group, catch loop of last double crochet and draw through first double crochet, tighten stitch.

Post stitch is worked as follows: Double crochet from back on wrong side rows and from front on right side rows under posts of stitches in row below.

Body of Blanket
Foundation row: Chain 45, make 1 double crochet in 3rd chain from hook, 1 double crochet in each stitch across row.

Row 1: Chain 3 to turn, skip first stitch, make 1 double crochet in each stitch across row, ending with 1 double crochet in top of turning chain.

Rows 2 and 3: Repeat row 1.

Row 4: Chain 3 to turn, skip first stitch, make 1 double crochet in next stitch, (double crochet under post of next stitch, make 1 double crochet in each of next 3 stitches, double crochet under post of next stitch, double crochet in each of next 3 stitches, double crochet under post of next stitch), double crochet in each of next 10 stitches, make 1 popcorn in next stitch, double crochet in next 10 stitches. Repeat between ()'s, ending 1 double crochet in last stitch, 1 double crochet in top of turning chain.

Row 5: Chain 3 to turn, repeat between ()'s of row 4, double crochet in each of next 9 stitches, make 1 popcorn in next stitch, double crochet in next stitch, popcorn in next stitch, double crochet in next 9 stitches. Repeat between ()'s of row 4, ending 1 double crochet in last stitch, 1 double crochet in top of turning chain.

Row 6: Chain 3 to turn, repeat between ()'s of row 4, double crochet in each of next 8 stitches, make 1 popcorn in next stitch, double crochet in next 3 stitches, make 1 popcorn in next stitch, double crochet in next 8 stitches. Repeat between ()'s of row 4, ending 1 double crochet in last stitch, 1 double crochet in top of turning chain.

Row 7: Chain 3 to turn, repeat between ()'s of row 4, double crochet in each of next 7 stitches, make 1 popcorn in next stitch, double crochet in each of next 5 stitches, make 1 popcorn in next stitch, double crochet in each of next 7 stitches. Repeat between ()'s of row 4, ending 1 double crochet in last stitch, 1 double crochet in top of turning chain.

Row 8: Chain 3 to turn, repeat between ()'s of row 4, double crochet in each of next 6 stitches, make 1 popcorn in next stitch, double crochet in

aran isle
baby blanket

each of next 3 stitches, make 1 popcorn in next stitch, double crochet in each of next 3 stitches, make 1 popcorn in next stitch, double crochet in each of next 6 stitches. Repeat between ()'s of row 4, ending with 1 double crochet last stitch, 1 double crochet top of turning chain.

Row 9: Chain 3 to turn, repeat between ()'s of row 4, double crochet in each of next 5 stitches, make 1 popcorn in next stitch, double crochet in each of next 3 stitches, make 1 popcorn in next stitch, double crochet in next stitch, make 1 popcorn in next stitch, double crochet in each of next 3 stitches, make 1 popcorn in next stitch, double crochet in each of next 5 stitches. Repeat between ()'s of row 4, ending with 1 double crochet in last stitch, 1 double crochet in top of turning chain.

Row 10: Chain 3 to turn, repeat between ()'s of row 4, double crochet in each of next 4 stitches, make 1 popcorn in next stitch, double crochet in each of next 3 stitches, make 1 popcorn in next stitch, double crochet in each of next 3 stitches, make 1 popcorn in next stitch, double crochet in each of next 3 stitches, make 1 popcorn in next stitch, double crochet in each of next 4 stitches. Repeat between ()'s of row 4, ending with 1 double crochet in last stitch, 1 double crochet in top of turning chain.

Row 11: Chain 3 to turn, repeat between ()'s of row 4, double crochet in each of next 3 stitches, make 1 popcorn in next stitch, double crochet in each of next 3 stitches, make 1 popcorn in next stitch, double crochet in each of next 5 stitches, make 1 popcorn in next stitch, double crochet in each of next 3 stitches, make 1 popcorn in next stitch, double crochet in each of next 3 stitches. Repeat between ()'s of row 4, ending with 1 double crochet in last stitch, 1 double crochet in top of turning chain.

Rows 12−18: Repeat rows 10−4 in that order.

Row 19: Repeat between ()'s of row 4, double crochet in next 21 stitches, repeat between ()'s of row 4, ending with 1 double crochet in last stitch, 1 double crochet in top of turning chain.

Rows 20 and 21: Repeat row 19.

Rows 22−36: Repeat rows 4−18.

Rows 37−39: Repeat rows 1−3. End off.

Finishing

Joining yarn in any corner, chain 3, make 2 more double crochets in same corner space, work double crochet along side of blanket, working 2 double crochets in each row. Make 3 double crochets in corner to turn, continue to double crochet along bottom, making 1 double crochet in each stitch. Make 3 double crochets in corner, continue down other side, making 2 double crochets in each row. Make 3 double crochets in corner to turn, continue along top of blanket, making 1 double crochet in each stitch, end off.

To make fringe: Cut a piece of cardboard 8 inches (20 cm) long. Wrap yarn about 20 times around cardboard. Cut 1 end only. Take 2 strands of yarn just cut, fold in half. Using crochet hook, pull the 2 strands through a stitch, forming a loop about 1 inch (2.5 cm), then draw loose ends through loop. Continue to wrap yarn and fringe all around blanket, using 2 strands for each fringe.

Do not block.

woman's ribbon-tied vest

The unique use of the ribbon yarn
to make little bows throughout
the garment gives this vest a truly
unusual look. It's very easy to
make, even for beginners.

Women's Sizes
Directions are for size 8. Changes for size 10 and 12 are in parentheses.

Materials
5 rolls (100 yds or 92 m each) Ribbon by Gemini Innovations—2 rolls in
Main Color, 1 roll each in Colors A, B, C—or any yarn to give gauge
gauge

Hook   **Gauge**

Size 10 or J   2½ stitches = 1 inch (2.5 cm)

Striping Pattern

Rows 1–8: Work in Main Color
Rows 9–14: Work in Color A
Rows 15–20: Work in Color B
Rows 21–26: Work in Color C
Rows 27–42: Work in Main Color
   Repeat for striping pattern.

Back

With Main Color, chain 45 (48, 51).
Foundation row: Work 1 single crochet in 2nd chain from hook, work 1 single crochet in each stitch to end of row.
Row 1: Chain 1 to turn, skip first stitch [chain-1 counts as first stitch], make 1 single crochet in each stitch to end of row [44 (47, 50) single crochets].
   Repeat row 1, following striping pattern, till piece is 9 (10, 11) inches (22.5, 25, 27.5 cm). Still following striping pattern, slip stitch over 2 stitches, work to within 2 stitches of other side, chain 1, and turn. Decrease 1 stitch each side, every row, 3 times. Keeping to pattern as established, work even till armhole is 8 (8½, 9) inches (20, 21.3, 22.5 cm), end off.

Left Front

With Main Color, chain 23 (24, 25). Work foundation row and row 1 same as for back. Following striping pattern, repeat row 1 till armhole, ending at arm side. Slip stitch over 3 stitches, finish row. Continuing in pattern, decrease 1 stitch arm side, every row, 3 times, *and, at the same time*, decrease 1 stitch at neck edge, every other row, till 5 (6, 7) stitches remain. Work even till same as back to shoulder, end off.

Right Front

Work same as for left front, reversing all shaping.

Finishing

Sew shoulder seams, sew underarm seams. Using Main Color, work 2 rows single crochet around armholes.
   Starting at bottom right, *work border as follows:*
Row 1: Single crochet up right front, around neckline, and down left front, chain 1, turn.
Row 2: Skip first stitch, work a 2nd row of single crochet all around, making 5 buttonholes, evenly spaced on right front, from V shaping to bottom [*to make buttonholes:* chain 2, skip 1 stitch].
Row 3: Chain 1, turn, skip first stitch, make a 3rd row of single crochet all around, making 1 stitch in buttonhole loop, end off.
   Cut 40 6-inch (15-cm) lengths from all colors, tie bows at random all over vest.
   Do not block.

56

Toddlers' Sizes

Directions are for size 2. Changes for sizes 3 and 4 are in parentheses.

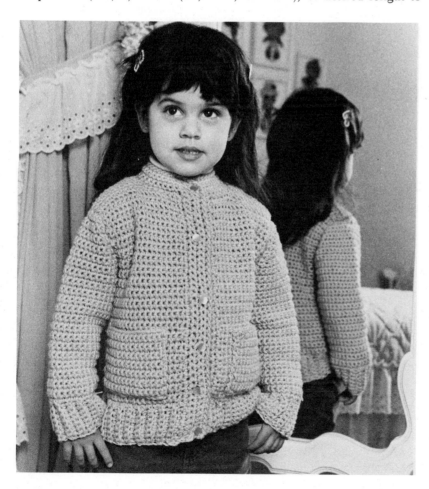

Materials

5 (5, 6) skeins (1¾ oz or 50 g each) Domani by Angora Corporation of America, or any baby yarn to give gauge
6 buttons

Hook	Gauge
Size 10 or J	3 stitches = 1 inch (2.5 cm)

Note: Yarn is used double strand throughout.

Back

Chain 8.

Foundation row: Make 1 single crochet in 2nd chain from hook, 1 single crochet in each chain to end of row [7 (7, 7) single crochets].

Row 1: Chain 1, turn, skip first stitch [chain-1 counts as first stitch], make 1 single crochet from back loop in next stitch, 1 single crochet from back loop in each stitch to end of row.

Repeat row 1 till you have worked 34 (36, 38) rows. Working along long end of border just worked, pick up 1 single crochet in each row [34 (36, 38) single crochets]. Continue working in single crochet from both loops till 8 (8½, 9) inches (20, 21.3, 22.5 cm), or desired length to

This classic child's cardigan, crocheted in single crochet, with great big pockets, is a perennial favorite.

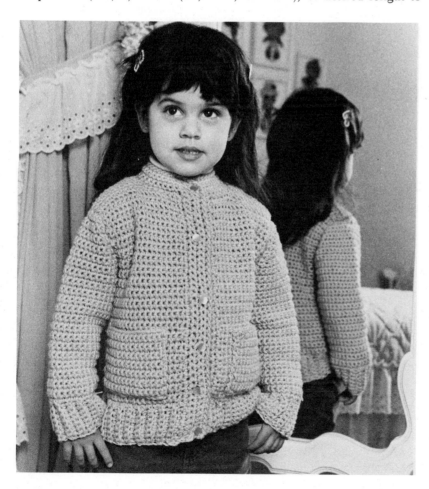

This classic child's cardigan, crocheted in single crochet, with great big pockets, is a perennial favorite.

57

underarm. Slip stitch over 2 stitches, work to within 2 stitches of other side, chain 1, and turn. Work even on 30 (32, 34) stitches till armhole is 4½ (5, 5½) inches (11.3, 12.5, 13.8 cm), end off.

Left Front
Chain 8. Work foundation row and row 1 same as for back. Continue to repeat row 1 till 18 (19, 20) rows have been worked. Working along long end of border just worked, pick up 18 (19, 20) stitches. Continue working in single crochet from both loops till same as back to armhole. Shape arm side same as for back. Keeping front edge even, work till armhole is 3 (3½, 4) inches (7.5, 8.8, 10 cm), ending at front edge. Slip stitch over 5 stitches, then decrease 1 stitch neck edge, every row, 3 times. Work even on remaining 8 (9, 10) stitches till shoulder, end off.

Right Front
Work same as for left front, reversing all shaping.

Sleeves
Chain 8. Work foundation row and row 1 same as for back. Continue to repeat row 1 till 20 (22, 24) rows have been worked. Working along long end of border just worked, pick up 1 single crochet in each row. On next row, working in single crochet from both loops, increase 1 stitch at beginning and end of row [22, (24, 26) single crochets in all]. Continue to work in pattern as established, increasing 1 stitch each side, every 1½ inches (3.8 cm), 3 times [28, (30, 32) stitches]. Work even till sleeve is 8½ (9, 9½) inches (21.3, 22.5, 23.8 cm). Slip stitch over 2 stitches, work to within 2 stitches of other side, chain 1, and turn. Continue as established, decreasing 1 stitch each side every other row, 5 (5, 6) times, end off.

Pockets (make 2)
Chain 17.
Foundation row: Make 1 single crochet in 2nd chain from hook, 1 single crochet in each stitch to end of row.
Row 1: Chain 1, turn, skip first stitch [chain-1 counts as first stitch], make 1 single crochet in next stitch, 1 single crochet in each stitch to end of row.
Repeat row 1 till pocket is 3 inches (7.5 cm), end off.

Finishing
Sew shoulder seams. Sew underarm seams. Set in sleeves. Sew in pockets.
Work border as follows:
Row 1: Starting at bottom right corner, work single crochet up front to neckline, make 3 single crochets in corner. Continue around neckline, make 3 single crochets in corner. Continue to bottom of left side, chain 1, turn. Continue to repeat row 1, 4 times more, making 6 buttonholes on 3rd row (right side for girls, left side for boys) [*to make buttonholes:* chain 2, skip 1 stitch], on next row, make 1 single crochet in buttonhole loop.
Sew on buttons. Do not block.

58

man's wrap cardigan

The man's wrap cardigan is made in sections up to the yoke, then joined and worked as one piece. The deep shawl collar and belt add to the sporty, casual look.

Men's Sizes

Directions are for size 36–38. Changes for sizes 40–42 and 44–46 are in parentheses.

Materials

16 (17, 18) skeins (3½ oz or 100 g each) Aspen by Brunswick—13 (14, 15) in Main Color, 1 skein each in Colors A, B, and C—or any bulky yarn to give gauge

Hooks

Size 10½ or K
Size P

Striping Pattern for Yoke

Rows 1–4: Work in Color A.
Rows 5 and 6: Work in Color B.
Rows 7–10: Work in Color C.

Gauge

1½ stitches = 1 inch (2.5 cm)

Back

With larger hook and Main Color chain 31 (34, 37).
Foundation row: Work 1 single crochet in 2nd chain from hook, 1 single crochet in each stitch across row [30 (33, 36) single crochets].
Row 1: Chain 1, turn, skip first stitch [chain-1 counts as first stitch], work 1 single crochet in each stitch to end of row.

Repeat row 1 till 16 (17, 18) inches (40, 42.5, 45 cm), or desired length to underarm. Break yarn and set this section aside.

59

Left Front

With larger hook and Main Color, chain 20 (21, 22). Work same as for back till armhole, set aside.

Right Front

Work same as for left front.

Sleeves

With size P larger hook and Main Color chain 15 (15, 16). Work foundation row and row 1 same as for back. Continue to repeat row 1, increasing 1 stitch each side, every 2½ inches (6 cm), 5 (6, 6) times. Work even till sleeve is 17 (17½, 18) inches (42.5, 43.8, 45 cm), end off. Set aside.

Yoke

Row 1 (joining row): Join Color A to top front edge of right front. Using larger hook, make single crochets across right front. Continue single crocheting across top of 1 sleeve, back, other sleeve, left front [all sections are now joined]. Mark beginning and end of each section with colored thread for decreasing.

Row 2 (first decrease row): Chain 1, turn, decrease 1 stitch at beginning and end of front, 1 stitch at beginning and end of sleeve, at beginning and end of back, at beginning and end of other sleeve, at beginning and end of remaining front [10 decreases made in all].

Row 3: Chain 1, turn, make 1 single crochet in 2nd stitch [chain-1 counts as first stitch], 1 single crochet in each stitch across row.

Working striping pattern of yoke, continue to repeat rows 2 and 3. When striping pattern is completed, join Main Color, and continue to repeat rows 2 and 3 for 10 (10, 12) rows more, end off.

Collar

With smaller hook, chain 7.

Foundation row: Work 1 single crochet from back loop in 2nd chain from hook, 1 single crochet from back loop in each stitch to end of row.

Row 1: Chain 1, turn, skip first stitch [chain-1 counts as first stitch], work 1 single crochet from back loop in next stitch, work 1 single crochet from back loop in each stitch across row [6 single crochets].

Continue to repeat row 1 till same length as front to yoke. Mark 1 side for inside edge. Then, continuing in same pattern as established, increase 1 stitch at inside edge only, every row, 7 times. Continue working on all stitches till 30 (30, 31) inches (75, 75, 77.5 cm) from marker. Continue, decreasing 1 stitch same side, every row, 7 times. Work even till same length as other side, end off.

Belt

With smaller hook, chain 6. Work foundation row and row 1 same as for collar. Repeat row 1 till desired length, end off.

Finishing

Sew underarm seams. Fold collar in half, center at back of neck. Pin in place, pinning at bottom and at neck shaping. Sew in place, sewing shaped side to garment. Chain 10 for each belt loop and tack in place.

Do not block.

woman's wrap cardigan

This wrap cardigan is made in sections up to the yoke, then joined and worked in one piece. The deep shawl collar and the curly textured yarn give it a very luxurious look. The easy stitch, which is done on a very large hook, is sure to make this project a favorite.

Women's Sizes

Directions are for small size. Changes for medium and large sizes are in parentheses.

Materials

20 (20, 21) skeins (1¾ oz or 50 g each) Tiffany by Stanley Berocco, or any loop yarn to give gauge

Hooks
Size 10½ or K
Size P

Gauge
1½ stitches = 1 inch (2.5 cm)

Note: Yarn is worked triple strand throughout.

Back

With larger hook, chain 27 (31, 34).

Foundation row: Make 1 single crochet in 2nd chain from hook, 1 single crochet in each stitch across row [26 (30, 33) single crochets].

Row 1: Chain 1, turn, skip first stitch [chain-1 counts as first stitch], make 1 single crochet in each stitch to end of row.

Repeat row 1 till 15 (16, 17) inches (37.5, 40, 42.5 cm), or desired length to underarm. Break yarn and set aside.

Left Front

With larger hook, chain 19 (20, 21). Work same as for back to armhole, set aside.

Right Front

Work same as for left front.

Sleeves

With larger hook, chain 14 (14, 15). Work foundation row and row 1 same as for back. Continue to repeat row 1, increasing 1 stitch each side, every 2 inches (5 cm), 5 (6, 6) times. Work even till sleeve is 16 (16½, 17) inches (40, 41.3, 42.5 cm), or desired length to underarm. End off, set aside.

Yoke

Row 1 (joining row): Join yarn to top front edge of right front. Using size larger hook, single crochet across right front, continue to single crochet across top of sleeve, back, other sleeve, and left front [all sections are now joined]. Mark beginning and end of each section with colored thread for decreasing.

Row 2 (first decrease row): Chain 1, turn. Decrease 1 stitch at beginning and end of front, 1 stitch at beginning and end of sleeve, at beginning and end of back, at the beginning and end of other sleeve, at beginning and end of remaining front [10 decreases made in all].

Row 3: Chain 1, turn. Work 1 single crochet in 2nd stitch [chain-1 counts as first stitch], 1 single crochet in each stitch across row.

Continue to repeat rows 2 and 3   9 (10, 10) times more, end off.

Collar

With smaller hook, chain 7.

Foundation row: Make 1 single crochet from back loop in 2nd chain from hook, 1 single crochet from back loop in each stitch to end of row.

Row 1: Chain 1, turn, skip first stitch [chain-1 counts as first stitch], make 1 single crochet from back loop in next stitch, make 1 single crochet from back loop in each stitch across row [6 single crochets].

Continue to repeat row 1 till same length as front to yoke. Mark 1 side for inside edge. Then, continuing in same pattern as established, increase 1 stitch at inside edge only, every row, 7 times. Continue working on all stitches till 29 (30, 30) inches (72.5, 75, 75 cm) from marker. Continue, decreasing 1 stitch same side, every row, 7 times. Work even till same length as other side, end off.

Belt

With smaller hook, chain 6. Work foundation row and row 1 same as for collar. Repeat Row 1 till desired length, end off.

Finishing

Sew underarm seams. Fold collar in half. Center at back of neck. Pin in place, pinning at bottom, start of neck shaping, and center back. Sew in place, sewing shaped side to garment. Chain 10 for each belt loop and tack in place. Do not block.

Women's Sizes

Directions are for small size. Changes for medium and large sizes are in parentheses.

Materials

12 (13, 13) skeins (3½ oz or 100 g each) Creole Cotton by Tahki
10 (11, 11) skeins in Main Color, 1 skein each in Colors A and B—or any cotton yarn to give gauge
6 assorted seashells

Hooks

Size 10½ or K
Size N

Gauge

2 double crochets = 1 inch (2.5 cm)

Back

With larger hook, chain 45 (48, 51).
Foundation row: Starting in 3rd chain from hook, make 1 double crochet in each chain to end of row [42 (45, 48) double crochets].

woman's beach cover-up

This colorful cotton cover-up, perfect for tossing over a bathing suit, is quick, easy, and fun to make. Seashells dangling from the neck ties give it a whimsical look. (For a matching cover-up in girls' sizes, see page 65.)

Row 1: Chain 2 to turn, skip first stitch [chain-2 counts as first stitch], make 1 double crochet in each stitch to end of row, make 1 double crochet in top of turning chain.

Repeat row 1 till 20 (21, 22) inches (50, 52.5, 55 cm), or desired length to underarm. Mark with colored thread for armhole, then continue in pattern as established for 7½ (8, 8½) inches (18.8, 20, 21.3 cm) more, end off.

Left Front
With larger hook, chain 24 (27, 30). Work same as for back till 4½ (5, 5½) inches (11.3, 12.5, 12.5 cm) above armhole marker, ending at neck edge. Slip stitch over 10 stitches, then decrease 1 stitch at neck edge, every row, 2 (4, 6) times. Work even on remaining 9 (10, 11) stitches until same as for back to shoulder, end off.

Sleeves
With larger hook, chain 33 (35, 37). Work same as for back till 14 (15, 16) inches (35, 37.5, 40 cm), end off.

Pockets *(make 2)*
Foundation row: With Main Color and larger hook, chain 4, join with slip stitch to form ring.
Row 1: Chain 4 [counts as 1 double crochet], make 11 more double crochets in ring, join with slip stitch to top of chain-4. Break off Main Color.
Row 2: Join Color A in any space between 2 double crochets, chain 4 [this counts as 1 double crochet], make 2 more double crochets in same space [this is half a corner], *skip 3 double crochets, chain 1, make 3 double crochets in next space, chain 1, make 3 double crochets in same space, repeat from * twice, skip 3 double crochets, chain 1, make 3 double crochets in same space that you began, chain 1, join with slip stitch to top of chain-4 [this completes corner].
Row 3: Chain 3, make 2 more double crochets in same space from which chain-3 is coming [this is half corner], *chain 1, make 3 double crochets in next chain-1 space, make 3 double crochets, chain 1, make 3 double crochets all in next corner space, repeat from * twice, chain 1, make 3 double crochets in next chain-1 space, chain 1, make 3 double crochets in same space that you started in, chain 1, join with slip stitch to top of chain-4, break off Color A.
Row 4: Join Color B in any corner space, chain 4, make 2 more double crochets in same space [this is half a corner] *chain 1, make 3 double crochets in next chain-1 space, chain 1, make 3 double crochets in next chain-1 space, chain 1, make 3 double crochets, chain 1, make 3 double crochets all in next corner space, repeat from * twice, chain 1, make 3 double crochets in next chain-1 space, chain 1, make 3 double crochets in next chain-1 space, chain 1, make 3 double crochets in same space that you started in, chain 1, join with slip stitch to top of starting chain-4, end off, leaving a long end for sewing pocket to garment.

Ties *(make 1 in each color)*
Using smaller hook, chain 100. End off.

Finishing

Sew shoulder seams. Fold sleeves in half and pin center top to shoulder seam. Pin into armhole, having each end meet the underarm marker. Sew in place. Sew underarm seams.

To make front border: Starting at bottom right front, using smaller hook, make 1 row single crochet along right front edge to neck, make 3 single crochets in corner stitch to turn. Continue single crocheting along neckline, make 3 single crochets in corner to turn, continue down left front. Chain 1, turn. Work a 2nd row of single crochet up left front to neckline, chain 2, then continue in double crochet along neck stitches, make single crochets down right front. Chain 1, turn. Repeat first border row, end off. Weave 3 ties in and out of the double crochet row at neck. Tie seashell at end of each tie. Do not block.

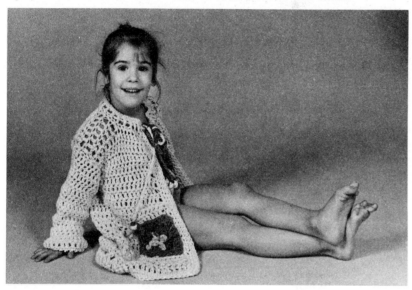

girl's beach cover-up

A beach cover-up just like mother's (see page 63) is sure to please any little girl. Colorful patch pockets and shells decorate this easy-to-make project.

Girls' Sizes

Directions are for size 4. Sizes for size 6 and 8 are in parentheses.

Materials

7 (7, 8) skeins (3½ oz or 100 g each) Creole Cotton by Tahki—5 (5, 6) skeins in Main Color, 1 skein each in Colors A and B—or any cotton yarn to give gauge
6 assorted seashells

Hooks
Size 10½ or K
Size N

Gauge
2 double crochets = 1 inch (2.5 cm)

Back

With larger hook, chain 31 (34, 37).
Foundation row: Starting in 3rd chain from hook, make 1 double crochet in each chain to end of row [28 (31, 34) double crochets].
Row 1: Chain 2 to turn, skip first stitch [chain-2 counts as first stitch], make 1 double crochet in each stitch to end of row, make 1 double crochet in top of turning chain.
  Repeat row 1 till 13 (14, 15) inches (32.5, 35, 37.5 cm), or desired

length to underarm. Mark with colored thread for armhole, then continue in pattern as established for 6 (6½, 7) inches (15, 16.3, 17.5 cm) more, end off.

Left Front
With larger hook, chain 17 (20, 23). Work same as for back till 3 (3½, 4) inches (7.5, 9, 10 cm) from armhole marker, ending at neck edge. Slip stitch over 6 (7, 8) stitches, then decrease 1 stitch at neck edge, every row, 2 (3, 4) times. Work even on remaining 6 (7, 8) stitches until same as for back to shoulder, end off.

Sleeves
With larger hook, chain 27 (29, 31). Work same as for back till 11 (11½, 12) inches (27.5, 28.8, 30 cm), end off.

Pockets (make 2)
Foundation row: With Main Color and larger hook, chain 4, join with slip stitch to form ring.
Row 1: Chain 4 [counts as 1 double crochet], make 11 more double crochets in ring, join with slip stitch to top of chain-4. Break off Main Color.
Row 2: Join Color A in any space between 2 double crochets, chain 4 [this counts as 1 double crochet], make 2 more double crochets in same space [this is half a corner], *skip 3 double crochets, chain 1, make 3 double crochets in next space, chain 1, make 3 double crochets in same space, repeat from * twice, skip 3 double crochets, chain 1, make 3 double crochets in same space that you began, chain 1, join with slip stitch to top of chain-4 [this completes corner]. Break Color A.
Row 3: Join Color B in any corner space, chain 3, make 2 more double crochets in same space from which chain-3 is coming [this is half corner], *chain 1, make 3 double crochets in next chain-1 space, make 3 double crochets, chain 1, make 3 double crochets all in next corner space, repeat from * twice, chain 1, make 3 double crochets in next chain-1 space, chain 1, make 3 double crochets in same space that you started in, chain 1, join with slip stitch to top of chain-4, break off, leaving a long thread to sew pocket to garment.

Ties (make 1 in each color)
Using smaller hook, chain 80, end off.

Finishing
Sew shoulder seams. Fold sleeves in half and pin center top to shoulder seam. Pin into armhole, having each end meet the underarm marker. Sew in place. Sew underarm seams.

To make front border: starting at bottom right front, using smaller hook, make 1 row single crochet along right front edge to neck, make 3 single crochets in corner stitch to turn. Continue single crocheting along neckline, make 3 single crochets in corner to turn, continue down left front. Chain 1, turn, work a 2nd row of single crochet up left front to neckline, chain 2, then continue in double crochet along neck stitches only, make single crochets down right front. Chain 1, turn. Repeat first border row, end off. Weave 3 ties in and out of double crochet row at neck. Tie seashells at end of each tie. Do not block.

66

woman's curly-sleeve jacket

The combination of curly and smooth textures gives this jacket a unique look. The entire jacket is done in simple single crochet.

Women's Sizes

Directions are for small size. Changes for medium and large sizes are in parentheses.

Materials

7 (8, 9) skeins (1¾ oz or 50 g each) Skol by Unger, or any worsted weight yarn to give gauge
7 (8, 9) skeins (1¾ oz or 50 g each) Caprice by Unger, or any curly yarn to give gauge
6 buttons

Hook   Gauge

Size N   2 stitches = 1 inch (2.5 cm)

Note: Curly yarn is used single strand; worsted yarn is used double strand throughout.

67

Back

With worsted yarn, chain 33 (35, 37).

Foundation row: Make 1 single crochet in 2nd chain from hook, make 1 single crochet in each chain across row [32 (34, 36) single crochets].

Row 1: Chain 1, turn, skip first stitch [chain-1 counts as first stitch], make 1 single crochet in each stitch across row, make 1 single crochet in top of turning chain.

Repeat row 1 till 10 (11, 12) inches (25, 27.5, 30 cm), or desired length to armhole. Slip stitch over 2 stitches, work to within 2 stitches of other side, chain 1, turn. Continuing in pattern as established, decrease 1 stitch each side, every row, 2 times. Work even on remaining 24 (26, 28) stitches till armhole is 6½ (7, 7½) inches (16.3, 17.5, 18.8 cm), end off.

Left Front

With worsted yarn, chain 17 (18, 19). Work foundation row and row 1 same as for back. Repeat row 1 till same length as back to armhole, end at arm side. Slip stitch over 2 stitches, complete row. Continue in pattern as established, decreasing 1 stitch at arm edge, every row, 2 times. Work even till armhole is 4½ (5, 5½) inches (11.3, 12.5, 13.8 cm), ending at neck edge. Slip stitch over 4 stitches, complete row. Continuing in pattern, decrease 1 stitch at neck edge, every row, 2 times. Work even on remaining 6 (7, 8) stitches, until same as back to shoulder, end off.

Right Front

Work same as for left front, reversing all shaping.

Sleeves

With curly yarn, chain 21 (22, 23). Work foundation row and row 1 same as for back. Repeat row 1 for 5 inches (12.5 cm). Increase 1 stitch each side and repeat this increase every 5 inches (12.5 cm), 1 (1, 2) time(s) more. Work even till sleeve is 14 (15, 16) inches (35, 37.5, 40 cm), or desired length to underarm. Slip stitch over 2 stitches, work to within 2 stitches of other side, chain 1, turn, then decrease 1 stitch each side, every row, 2 times. Work even till 6 (6½, 7) inches (15, 16.3, 17.5 cm) above armhole. Next row, work 2 single crochets together all across row, end off.

Finishing

Sew shoulder seams. Set in sleeves. Sew underarm seams.

To make trim: With curly yarn, starting at bottom right underarm seam, make single crochets all around entire garment, always making 3 single crochets in each corner to turn. Join with slip stitch to beginning stitch. Work 2 more rows the same [it is not necessary to make buttonholes, as buttons can easily fit through the loose crochet stitches]. With worsted yarn work 3 rows single crochet around bottom of sleeves, pulling in to fit wrist.

Sew on 6 buttons, evenly spaced. Do not block.

Teen Boys' Sizes

Directions are for size 16. Changes for size 18 and 20 are in parentheses.

Materials

7 (8, 9) skeins (1¾ oz or 50 g each) Derby by Unger, or any bulky tweed to give gauge

7 (8, 9) skeins (1¾ oz or 50 g each) Allora by Fantacia, or any worsted weight yarn to give gauge

Hooks	Gauge
Size 9 or I	2 stitches = 1 inch (2.5 cm) with tweed yarn
Size 10½ or K	2½ stitches = 1 inch (2.5 cm) with worsted yarn

teen boy's saddle-shoulder pullover

The interesting saddle shoulder and the combination of solid and tweed yarn give this sweater a very distinctive look.

Note: The bulky tweed is used single strand throughout, the worsted is used double strand throughout.

Back

With smaller hook and tweed yarn, chain 9.

Foundation row: Work 1 single crochet in 2nd chain from hook, 1 single crochet in each stitch across row [8 stitches].

Row 1: Chain 1 to turn, skip first stitch [chain-1 counts as first stitch], make 1 single crochet from back loop in next stitch, make 1 single crochet from back loop in each stitch to end of row.

Repeat row 1 till 32 (34, 36) rows have been worked, do not break yarn. Working along long edge of border just worked, pick up 1 single crochet in each row [32 (34, 36) single crochets]. Change to larger hook, continue to work single crochet through both loops till back is 13 (13½, 14) inches (32.5, 33.8, 35 cm) from beginning, or desired length to underarm. Slip stitch over 2 stitches, work to within 2 stitches of other side, chain 1, turn. Continue as established, decreasing 1 stitch each side, every row, 2 times. Work even on remaining 24 (26, 28) stitches until armhole is 6½ (7, 7½) inches (16.3, 17.5, 18.8 cm), end off.

Front

Work same as for back till armhole is 3 inches (7.5 cm). Work across 9 (10, 11) stitches, chain 1, and turn. Working on these stitches only, decrease 1 stitch at neck edge, every row, 3 times. Work even on remaining 6 (7, 8) stitches till armhole is 5½ (6, 6½) inches (13.8, 15, 16.3 cm), end off. Skip center 6 stitches, join yarn at neck edge, and work remaining 9 (10, 11) stitches to correspond, end off.

Sleeves

With worsted yarn and smaller hook, chain 9. Work foundation row and row 1 same as for back for 20 (22, 24) rows, do not break yarn. Working along long end of border just made, pick up 26 (28, 30) stitches. Change to larger hook and work single crochet through both loops, increasing 1 stitch each side, every 3 inches (7.5 cm), 4 times. Work even till sleeve is 15½ (16, 16½) inches (38.8, 40, 41.3 cm), or desired length to underarm. Slip stitch over 2 stitches, work to within 2 stitches of other side, chain 1, turn. Continue as established, decreasing 1 stitch each side, every row, till 10 stitches remain. Work even for 3 (3½, 3½) inches (7.5, 8.8, 8.8 cm) more, end off.

Collar

With worsted yarn and smaller hook, chain 7. Work foundation row and row 1 same as for back for 23 (23½, 24) inches (57.5, 58.8, 59 cm), end off.

Finishing

Sew underarm seams. Pin sleeve in place, having tab at top of sleeve form saddle shoulder. Sew sleeve in place. Center collar at back of neck, pin collar in place, having short ends of collar overlap, left over right, at front. Sew collar in place. Do not block.

70

woman's ribbon camisole

This dressy little camisole, to be worn by itself or paired with the Woman's Shell Jacket (see page 72), is a snap to make. When it is all finished, weave shiny, satin ribbon through the open mesh stitches and tie into perky little bows.

Women's Sizes

Directions are for size 8. Changes for sizes 10 and 12 are in parentheses.

Materials

3 (3, 3) skeins (1²/₅ oz or 40 g each) Dolly by Unger, or any bouclé yarn to give gauge
4 yards (3.6 m) satin ribbon, ½ inch (1.3-cm) width
2 yards (1.8 m) elastic cord

Hook
Size 10½ or K

Gauge
2½ stitches = 1 inch (2.5 cm)

Note: Yarn is used double strand throughout.

Back

Chain 44 (47, 50).
Foundation row: Make 1 single crochet in 2nd chain from hook, 1 single crochet in each stitch to end of row.
Row 1 (open mesh row): Chain 3 to turn, skip first stitch *double crochet in next stitch, chain 1, skip 1, repeat from * across row, ending with 1 double crochet in last stitch.
Row 2: Chain 1 to turn, make 2 single crochets in each chain-1 space across row, end 1 single crochet in turning chain.
Row 3: Chain 1 to turn, skip first stitch [chain-1 counts as first stitch], make 1 single crochet in each stitch to end of row.

Repeat row 3 till 3 inches (7.5 cm) of single crochet after open mesh row. Repeat from row 1, 2 times more [piece should be about 11½ inches (28.8 cm) long]. Repeat row 1. Repeat row 2. End off.

Front
Work same as for back.

Finishing
Sew side seams, making sure that open mesh rows meet. Cut ribbon into 1-yard (1-m) lengths, weave in and out of open mesh stitches, tying into bows at center front. Do not block.

woman's shell jacket

Women's Sizes
Directions are for size small. Changes for medium and large sizes are in parentheses.

Materials
10 (11, 12) skeins (1²/₅ oz or 40 g each) Dolly by Unger, or any bouclé yarn to give gauge

Hooks
Size 8 or H
Size 10½ or K

Gauge
2½ stitches = 1 inch (2.5 cm)

Note: Yarn is worked double strand throughout.

Back
With larger hook, chain 50 (56, 62).
Foundation row: Starting in 5th chain from hook, make 2 double crochets, chain 1, 2 double crochets all in same stitch [shell made], *skip 2 chains, 1 double crochet, chain 1, 1 double crochet in next chain [V stitch made], skip 2 chains, make 1 shell in next stitch, repeat from * across row, ending skip 2 chains, make 1 double crochet in last stitch [there will be 8 (9, 10) shells and 7 (8, 9) V stitches on row and 1 double crochet at each end].
Row 1: Chain 3 to turn, work 1 V stitch in chain-1 space of first shell, *make 1 shell in chain-1 space of next V stitch, make 1 V stitch in chain-1 space of next shell, repeat from * across row, ending with 1 double crochet in top of turning chain.
Row 2: Chain 3 to turn, work 1 shell in chain-1 space of first V stitch, *make 1 V stitch in chain-1 space of next shell, make 1 shell in chain-1 space of next V stitch, repeat from * across row, ending with 1 double crochet in top of turning chain.

Repeat rows 1 and 2 till 11 (11½, 12) inches (27.5, 28.8, 30 cm), or desired length to underarm. Slip stitch over 1 shell, work to within 1 shell of other side, chain 3, turn. Being sure to keep pattern as established, continue to work on center 6 (7, 8) shells until armhole is 7 (7½, 8) inches (17.5, 18.8, 20 cm), end off.

Left Front
With larger hook, chain 26 (26, 32). Work foundation and rows 1 and 2

72

same as for back [there will be 4 (4, 5) shells and 3 (3, 4) V stitches on row and 1 double crochet at each end].

Continue to repeat rows 1 and 2 till armhole, ending at arm side. Slip stitch over 1 shell, chain 3, and continue across row. Keeping front edge even, work till armhole is 5 (5½, 6) inches (12.5, 13.8, 15 cm), ending at front edge. Slip stitch over 2 shells and 1 V stitch, chain 3, finish row. Next row, decrease 1 stitch at neck edge, and repeat this decrease every row, 3 times. Work even to shoulder, end off.

Right Front
Work same as for left front, reversing all shaping.

Sleeves
With larger hook, chain 38 (38, 44). Work foundation row and rows 1 and 2 same as for back [there will be 6 (6, 7) shells and 5 (5, 6) V stitches on row]. Continue till sleeve is 6½ (7, 7½) inches (16.3, 17.5, 18.8 cm). Slip stitch over 1 shell, work to within 1 shell of other side, chain and turn. Continue on center patterns only till cap is 6½ (7, 7½) inches (16.3, 17.5, 18.8 cm). Next row, change to smaller hook, work in single crochets, working 2 stitches together all across row, end off.

Finishing
Sew shoulder seams, set in sleeves, being sure to center cap on shoulder seam. Sew underarm seams. With smaller hook, starting at bottom right corner, work single crochets up right front, make 3 single crochets in corner to turn, continue around neck, make 3 single crochets in corner to turn. Continue down left front, chain 1, turn. Repeat this row 2 times more, end off. Do not block.

The delicate shell stitch and textured bouclé yarn give this jacket a very airy look. Pop it over the Woman's Ribbon Camisole (see page 71) for a very special occasion.

man's sporty pullover

Men's Sizes
Directions are for size 38. Changes for size 40 and 42 are in parentheses.

Materials
16 (17, 18) skeins (2 oz or 60 g each) Aspen by Brunswick—14 skeins in Main Color, 1 skein each in Color A and Color B—or any bulky yarn to give gauge

Hooks
Size 10½ or K
Size N

Gauge
2 stitches = 1 inch (2.5 cm)

The "granny square" is always popular and has been used in many ways. Here three large grannies form the yoke of this great pullover for men.

Back
With smaller hook and Main Color, chain 10.
Foundation row: Make 1 single crochet in 2nd chain from hook, 1 single crochet in each stitch across row [9 single crochets].
Row 1: Chain 1 to turn, skip first stitch [chain-1 counts as first stitch], make 1 single crochet from back loop in next stitch, make 1 single crochet from back loop in each stitch across row.

Repeat row 1 for 40 (42, 44) rows [20 (21, 22) ridges]. Working along the long edge of border, work 1 single crochet in each row [40 (42, 44) single crochets]. Chain 1, turn. Continue to work in single crochet through both loops, using the larger hook, till back is 14 (14½, 15) inches (35, 36.3, 37.5 cm) from the beginning, or desired length to underarm. Mark at this point for underarm, then continue in single crochet for 8½ (9, 9½) inches (21.3, 22.5, 23.8 cm) more, end off.

Front
Work same as for back to underarm, set this piece aside.

Make 3 granny squares as follows (each square should be 7 inches (17.5 cm) square):
Foundation row: With Main Color and larger hook, chain 4, join with slip stitch to form ring.
Row 1: Chain 4 [counts as 1 double crochet], make 11 more double crochets in ring, join with slip stitch to top of chain-4, break off Main Color.
Row 2: Join Color A in any space between 2 double crochets, chain 4 [this counts as 1 double crochet], make 2 more double crochets in same space [this is half a corner], *skip 3 double crochets, chain 1, make 3 double crochets in next space, chain 1, make 3 double crochets in same space, repeat from * twice, skip 3 double crochets, chain 1, make 3 double crochets in same space that you began, chain 1, join with slip stitch to top of chain 4 [this completes corner]. Break off Color A.
Row 3: Join Color B in any corner space, chain 3, make 2 more double crochets in same space that chain-3 is coming from [this is half corner], *chain 1, make 3 double crochets in next chain-1 space, make 3 double crochets, chain 1, 3 double crochets all in next corner space, repeat from * twice, chain 1, make 3 double crochets in next chain-1 space, chain 1, make 3 double crochets in same space that you started in, chain 1, join with slip stitch to top of chain 4.

74

Rows 4–6: Still using Color B, chain 1, make 2 single crochets in same space chain 1 is coming from, *make 1 single crochet in each double crochet and 1 single crochet in each chain-1 space to corner, make 3 single crochets in corner space, repeat from *twice, make 1 single crochet in each stitch and each space to first corner, join with slip stitch, end off.

For size 42 only: Work 1 more row single crochet all around.

Sew 3 squares together, then sew to top of front section.

Top left front: Join Main Color at end of first square, work single crochet across first square, chain 1, turn, continue in single crochet on this section only, decrease 1 stitch at neck edge, every row, 6 (5, 4) times. Work even till same as back to shoulder, end off.

Top right front: Skip center square. Work right front same as left front, reversing all shaping.

Sleeves

With smaller hook, chain 10. Work foundation row and row 1 same as for back. Repeat row 1 for 24 (26, 28) rows. Work single crochet along the long end, picking up 1 stitch in each row [24 (26, 28) stitches]. Change to larger hook, work in single crochet from both loops, increasing 1 stitch each side, every 2 inches (5 cm), 6 (6, 7) times. Work even till sleeve is 18½ (19, 19½) inches (45.3, 47.5, 49 cm), or desired length, end off.

Finishing

Sew shoulder seams. Centering sleeves on shoulder seam and having end of sleeve meet armhole marker on back, and granny squares on front, set in sleeves. Sew underarm seams. With smaller hook, work 2 rows single crochet all around neck opening, end off. Do not block.

woman's bobble vest

Women's Sizes
Directions are for small size. Changes for medium and large sizes are in parentheses.

Materials
3 skeins (1¾ oz or 50 g each) Nadia by Fantacia, or any nubby textured yarn to give gauge
3 skeins (1²/₅ oz or 40 g each) Samida by Melrose—2 skeins in Color A, 1 skein in Color B—or any mohair to give gauge
4 cones (100 yards or 92 m each) Rayonette by Melrose—2 cones in a light shade, 2 cones in a dark shade—or any rayon chainette to give gauge
6 buttons

Hook
Size 10½ or K

Gauge
3 single crochets = 1 inch (2.5 cm)

Note: The rayon chainette is used double strand throughout.

Patterns
Popcorn stitch is worked as follows: Chain 3 to begin row *skip first stitch, make 5 double crochets in next stitch, take out hook and insert into first double crochet of the 5 just made, then pull dropped loop through this double crochet and complete stitch, chain 1, repeat from * across row, ending with 1 double crochet in last stitch.

Bobble stitch is worked as follows: Chain 3 to begin row *skip first stitch, [yarn over and pull up a long loop] 4 times, yarn over and pull through all but last loop on hook, yarn over and pull through 2, chain 1, repeat from * across row, ending with 1 double crochet in last stitch.

Back
With nubby yarn, chain 52 (55, 58).
Foundation row: Work 1 single crochet in 2nd chain from hook, 1 single crochet in each chain across row [51 (54, 57) single crochets].
Row 1: Chain 1 to turn, skip first stitch [chain-1 counts as first stitch], work 1 single crochet in each stitch to end of row.
Rows 2–4: Repeat row 1. Break yarn and join light shade of rayon yarn.
Rows 5 and 6: Repeat row 1. Do not break rayon yarn.
Row 7: With Color A of mohair, work 1 popcorn row.
Row 8: Chain 1, turn, work 2 single crochets in each chain-1 space across row, 1 single crochet in top of turning chain, break mohair.
Rows 9 and 10: With light shade of rayon yarn, repeat rows 5 and 6.
Rows 11–14: With nubby yarn, repeat rows 1–4.
Rows 15 and 16: With light shade of rayon yarn, repeat rows 5 and 6.
Row 17: With Color B of mohair, work 1 bobble stitch row.
Row 18: Repeat row 1. Break Color B of mohair.
Rows 19 and 20: With light shade of rayon yarn, repeat row 1. Break light shade of rayon yarn.
Rows 21–24: With nubby yarn, repeat rows 1–4.

This colorful vest, although not a beginner's project, is not as difficult as it appears to be. It's really just a combination of three simple stitches —single crochet, a puff stitch, and a bobble stitch.

Rows 25 and 26: With dark shade of rayon yarn, repeat rows 1 and 2. Do not break rayon yarn.

Row 27: With Color A of mohair, work 1 popcorn row.

Row 28: Repeat row 8. Break mohair.

Rows 29 and 30: With dark shade of rayon yarn, repeat rows 1 and 2. Break rayon yarn.

   Continuing in striping pattern as established, work till 11 (11½, 12) inches (27.5, 28.8, 30 cm), or desired length to underarm. Still keeping striping pattern as established, slip stitch over 3 stitches, work to within 3 stitches of other side, and turn. Decrease 1 stitch each side, every row, 3 times. Work even till armhole is 8 (8½, 9) inches (20, 21.3, 22.5 cm), end off.

Left Front
With nubby yarn, chain 27 (29, 31). Work foundation row and row 1 same as for back.
Continuing in same striping pattern as for back, work to armhole. Shape arm side same as for back, keep front edge even, work until armhole is 5 (5½, 6) inches (12.5, 13.8, 15 cm), ending at front edge.

Shape neck as follows: Slip stitch over 8 stitches, then decrease 1 stitch neck edge, every row, 4 times. Work even on remaining 8 (10, 12) stitches till same as back to shoulder, end off.

Right Front
Work same as for left front, reversing all shaping.

Finishing
Sew shoulder seams, sew underarm seams.

Work front border as follows:

Row 1: With nubby yarn, starting at right underarm seam, work single crochet along bottom to bottom right front, make 3 single crochets in corner, continue single crochet up right front to neck, make 3 single crochets in corner, continue along neckline to top of left front, make 3 single crochets in corner. Continue down left front, make 3 single crochets in corner, continue along bottom, back to where you started, join with a slip stitch, do not break nubby yarn.

Row 2: With light shade of rayon yarn, make a 2nd row of single crochet, still making 3 stitches in each corner, and making 6 evenly spaced buttonholes on right front [*to make buttonholes:* chain 2, skip 1 stitch].

Row 3: With nubby yarn, make a 3rd row of single crochet, still making 3 stitches in each corner, and making 1 single crochet in each chain-2 space of buttonholes, end off.

Do not block.

man's zippered jacket

Warm, practical, and easy to make, this man's jacket features a big collar and roomy pockets. It's a really simple project that looks great.

Men's Sizes
Directions are for size 36. Changes for size 38 and 40 are in parentheses.

Materials
8 (9, 10) skeins (3½ oz or 100 g each) Aspen by Brunswick, or any bulky yarn to give gauge
8 (9, 10) skeins (2 oz or 60 g each) Dji Dji by Stanley Berocco, or any brushed wool to give gauge
1 heavy-duty zipper

Hooks
Size 10½ or K
Size N

Gauge
2 stitches = 1 inch (2.5 cm)

Note: Use 1 strand of each yarn held together throughout.

Back
With larger hook, chain 39 (41, 43).
Foundation row: Make 1 single crochet in 2nd chain from hook, make

1 single crochet in each chain to end of row [38 (40, 42) single crochets].
Row 1: Chain 1 to turn, skip first stitch [chain-1 counts as first stitch], make 1 single crochet in next stitch, make 1 single crochet in each stitch across row.

Repeat row 1 till 14 (14½, 15) inches (35, 36.3, 37.5 cm) from beginning, or desired length to underarm. Slip stitch over 2 stitches, work to within 2 stitches of other side, chain and turn. Continue in single crochet till 8½ (9, 9½) inches (21.3, 22.5, 23.8 cm) above armhole, end off.

Left Front
With larger hook, chain 21 (22, 23) Work foundation row and row 1 same as for back. Repeat row 1 till same as for back to armhole. Shape armhole same as for back, keeping front edge even. Work till armhole is 6½ (7, 7½) inches (16.3, 17.5, 18.8 cm), ending at front edge.

Shape neck as follows: Slip stitch over 8 stitches, then decrease 1 stitch neck edge, every row, 4 times. Work even on remaining 6 (7, 8) stitches till same as back to shoulder, end off.

Right Front
Work same as for left front, reversing all shaping.

Sleeves
With smaller hook, chain 10.
Foundation row: Work 1 single crochet in 2nd chain from hook, 1 single crochet in each chain across row.
Row 1: Chain 1, turn, skip first stitch [chain-1 counts as first stitch], make 1 single crochet from back loop in next stitch, make 1 single crochet from back loop in each stitch across row.

Repeat row 1 for 24 (26, 28) rows. Working along long edge of border just made, work 1 single crochet in each row [24 (26, 28) single crochets]. Change to larger hook and continue working single crochet from both loops, increasing 1 stitch each side, every 2 inches (5 cm), 5 (5, 6) times. Work even till sleeve is 18½ (19, 19½) inches (45.3, 47.5, 49 cm), or desired length, end off.

Collar
With smaller hook, chain 12. Work foundation row and row 1 same as for sleeves. Repeat row 1 for 54 (56, 58) rows, end off.

Pockets *(make 2)*
With larger hook, chain 15 (16, 17). Work foundation row and row 1 same as for back. Repeat row 1 for 5 (5½, 6) inches (12.5, 13.8, 15 cm), end off.

Finishing
Sew pockets to each front, centering on front and placing 1 inch (2.5 cm) from bottom. Sew shoulder seams, set in sleeves, sew underarm seams. Work 2 rows single crochet along each front edge, using the smaller hook. Pin collar in place, centering at back of neck and having collar go right up to end of fronts. Sew zipper in place. Do not block.

Girls' Sizes

Directions are for size 4. Changes for sizes 6 and 8 are in parentheses.

Materials

11 (12, 13) skeins (1²/₅ oz or 40 g each) Samida by Melrose—2 (3, 3) skeins in purple, 1 skein in pink, 2 skeins in red, 2 (2, 3) skeins in orange, 1 skein in yellow, 2 skeins in green, and 1 skein in blue—or any mohair to give gauge

3 (3, 4) cones (100 yards or 92 m each) Rayonette by Melrose, or any rayon chainette to give gauge (black is recommended to set off the bright colors)

5 buttons

Hook	Gauge
Size 10½ or K	3 single crochets = 1 inch (2.5 cm)

Note: The rayon chainette is used double strand.

If the child is allergic to mohair or finds it uncomfortable, most knitting worsteds will give same gauge as mohair.

Patterns

Colors are used in the following sequence: Purple, pink, red, orange, yellow, green, and blue; they are always separated from one another by the black rayon chainette.

little girl's rainbow coat and hat set

What little girl wouldn't love this colorful coat that incorporates all the colors of the rainbow in a beautiful combination of stitches? It's fun to make and fun to wear.

Popcorn is worked as follows: Chain 3 to begin row, *skip first stitch, make 5 double crochets in next stitch, take out hook and insert into first double crochet of the 5 just made, then pull dropped loop through this double crochet and complete stitch, chain 1, repeat from * across row, ending with 1 double crochet in last stitch.

Puff stitch is worked as follows: Chain 3 to begin row, *skip first stitch, (yarn over and pull up a long loop) 4 times, yarn over and pull through 2, chain 1, repeat from * across row, ending with 1 double crochet in last stitch.

coat Back

With purple mohair, chain 52 (55, 58).

Foundation row: Make 1 single crochet in 2nd chain from hook, 1 single crochet in each chain across row [51 (54, 57) single crochets].

Row 1: Chain 1 to turn, skip first stitch [chain-1 counts as first stitch], work 1 single crochet in each stitch to end of row.

Rows 2–4: Repeat row 1. Break off purple yarn, join black rayon chainette.

Rows 5 and 6: Repeat row 1. Do not break rayon chainette, but carry up loosely all through garment.

Row 7: With pink mohair, work 1 popcorn row.

Row 8: With pink mohair, chain 1, turn, make 2 single crochets in each chain-1 space across row, 1 single crochet in top of turning chain, break off pink.

Rows 9 and 10: With rayon chainette, repeat rows 5 and 6.

Rows 11–14: With red mohair, repeat rows 1–4, break off red.

Rows 15 and 16: With rayon chainette, repeat rows 5 and 6.

Row 17: With orange mohair, work 1 puff stitch row.

Row 18: Repeat row 1, break off orange.

Rows 19 and 20: With rayon chainette, repeat rows 5 and 6.

Rows 21–24: With yellow mohair, repeat rows 1–4, break off yellow.

Rows 25 and 26: With rayon chainette, repeat rows 5 and 6.

Row 27: With green mohair, work 1 popcorn row.

Row 28: With green mohair, repeat row 8, break off green.

Rows 29 and 30: With rayon chainette, repeat rows 5 and 6.

Rows 31–34: With blue mohair, repeat rows 1–4, break off blue.

Rows 35 and 36: With rayon chainette, repeat rows 5 and 6.

Continuing to repeat the color sequence and the pattern as established, work until 12 (13, 14) inches (30, 32.5, 35 cm), or desired length to underarm. Slip stitch over 3 stitches, work to within 3 stitches other side, chain 1, turn, then decrease 1 stitch each side, every row, 3 times. Continue as established till armhole is 5½ (6, 6½) inches (13.8, 15, 16.3 cm), end off.

Left Front

With purple mohair, chain 27, 29, 31). Work foundation row and row 1 same as for back. Continuing in same color sequence and pattern same as for back, work to armhole. Shape arm side same as for back, keeping front edge even. Work till armhole is 3½ (4, 4½) inches (8.8, 10, 11.3 cm), ending at front edge.

Shape neck as follows: Slip stitch over 8 stitches then decrease 1 stitch neck edge, every row, 6 times. Work even on remaining 6 (8, 10) stitches to shoulder, end off.

Right Front

Work same as for left front, reversing all shaping.

Sleeves

With red mohair, chain 37 (39, 41). Starting with row 11, work color sequence and patterns same as for back, till 8 (9, 10) inches (20, 22.5, 25 cm), or desired length to underarm [it is desirable to start armhole on same color and stripe as back and front, so that patterns will meet when sewn together]. Slip stitch over 3 stitches, work to within 3 stitches of other side. Still working as established, decrease 1 stitch each side, every row, 3 times. Work even till cap of sleeve is 5½ (6, 6½) inches (13.8, 15, 16.3 cm). Next row, work single crochet, working 2 stitches together all across row, end off.

Finishing

Sew shoulder seams, set in sleeves. Sew underarm seams.

Work border as follows: Starting at bottom right underarm seam, with red, work 1 row single crochet all around garment, making 3 single crochets in each corner to turn, do not break red. Join rayon chainette, work a 2nd row of single crochet all around, making 5 evenly spaced buttonholes on right front, starting about 5 (5½, 6) inches (12.5, 13.8, 15 cm) from bottom [*to make buttonholes:* chain 2, skip 1 stitch], break off rayon chainette. Make a 3rd row of single crochet all around, with red, making 1 single crochet in each buttonhole space, end off.

Do not block.

hat

With purple mohair, chain 81 (83, 85). Work foundation row and row 1 same as for back of coat. Continue in color sequence and pattern same as for coat till row 18 is completed.

Row 19: With rayon chainette, work 1 row single crochet, working 2 stitches together all across row.

Row 20: Repeat row 19, break off rayon chainette, leaving a long end for sewing.

Finishing

Using the long end of rayon chainette, gather top of hat and firmly stitch down. Then, using same end, sew back seam.

Work bottom band as follows:

Row 1: With red mohair, make 1 row single crochet all around bottom of hat.

Row 2: With red mohair, make 1 row of single crochet, working every 4th and 5th stitch together, do not break off red.

Row 3: With rayon chainette, make 1 row of single crochet, working every 4th and 5th stitch together.

Row 4: With rayon chainette, make 1 row of single crochet, break off rayon chainette.

Rows 5 and 6: With red mohair, make 1 row of single crochet all around, end off.

man's
vertical-striped
pullover

Men's Sizes
Directions are for size 38. Changes for sizes 40 and 42 are in parentheses.

Materials
20 (21, 22) skeins (2 oz or 60 g each) Aspen by Brunswick—16 (17, 18) in Main Color, 2 skeins each in Colors A and B—or any bulky yarn to give gauge

Hooks
Size 10½ or K
Size N

Gauge
2 stitches = 1 inch (2.5 cm)

Striping Pattern
Rows 1–4: Work in Main Color.
Rows 5 and 6: Work in Color A.
Rows 7 and 8: Work in Color B.

Back
Starting at side of garment, with larger hook and Main Color, chain 28 (29, 30).
Foundation row: Make 1 single crochet in 2nd chain from hook, 1 single crochet in each stitch across row.
Row 1: Chain 1, turn, skip first stitch, make 1 single crochet in 2nd stitch, make 1 single crochet in each stitch to end of row, make 1 single crochet in top of turning chain.

Repeat row 1, following striping pattern, till piece measures 19 (20, 21) inches (47.5, 50, 52.5 cm) wide [it is desirable to end all pieces with 4 rows Main Color so that they will match when sewn together].

Front
Work same as for back.

Yoke and Sleeves
Starting at cuff of sleeve, with Main Color and larger hook, chain 23 (25, 27). Work foundation row and row 1 same as for back. Continue to repeat row 1, increasing 1 stitch each side, every 2½ inches (6 cm), 5 (6, 6) times, [32 (36, 38) stitches]. Place marker by last increase. Work even till sleeve is 17 (17½, 18) inches (42.5, 43.8, 45 cm), or desired length to underarm. Place another marker at this point. Work 5 inches (12.5 cm) past this 2nd marker.

Shape neck as follows: Chain 1, turn, work across 15 (17, 18) stitches, chain 1, turn. Working on these stitches only, work for 9 (10, 11) inches (22.5. 25, 27.5 cm), end off. Skip 2 stitches, join yarn, work remaining 15 (17, 18) stitches for 9 (10, 11) inches (22.5, 25, 27.5 cm), do not break yarn. Chain 2, join 2 sections together, end off.

Joining yarn at one side, and working all as one again, continue for 5 inches (12.5 cm) more. Place marker at this point. Now work to correspond to other side, decreasing instead of increasing on sleeve.

84

The unusual aspect of this interesting pullover is that the body is made from the side over and the yoke and sleeves are done together. Using this method, it is easy to create interesting color combinations.

Finishing

Sew back and front to yoke, matching sides to underarm markers. Sew underarm seams. With Main Color and smaller hook, work 3 rows single crochet around neck opening, pulling in slightly if necessary. Work 2 rows single crochet around bottom of sleeves. Do not block.

string placemats

Size
Approximately 9½ by 14 inches (23.8 by 35 cm)

Materials
1 cone (1 lb or 0.5 kg) packing cord

Hook
Size 8 or H

Gauge
2 double crochets, chain 1 = 1 inch (2.5 cm)

Body
Chain 34.

Foundation row: Make 1 double crochet in 4th chain from hook *chain 2, skip 2 chains, 1 double crochet in next stitch, repeat from * across row, ending with chain 2, 1 double crochet in last chain [12 open boxes].

Row 1: Chain 3, turn, make 2 double crochets in first open box * chain 1, 2 double crochets in next open box, repeat from * across ending with chain 1, 2 double crochets in last open box, 1 double crochet in 3rd stitch of turning chain [you will have 12 groups of double crochets, 1 double crochet each side].

Row 2: Chain 5, turn, make 1 double crochet in first chain-1 space, * chain 2, make 1 double crochet in next chain-1 space, repeat from * across row, ending with 1 double crochet in top of turning chain [12 boxes].

Repeat rows 1 and 2 for 13 inches (32.5 cm), ending with row 2.

Edging
Row 1: Join yarn in any space, work single crochet all around, making 3 single crochets in each corner to turn. Join with slip stitch to first stitch.

Row 2: Chain 3, make 1 puff stitch in the next stitch [*to make puff stitch:* yarn over hook 3 times, yarn over and through all stitches], *chain 1, make 1 puff stitch in next stitch, repeat from * all around, making 3 puff stitches in each corner stitch, join with slip stitch to top of beginning chain-3.

Row 3: Make 2 single crochets between each puff stitch, join with slip stitch to first stitch, end off.

The unusual feature of these placemats is that they are made with ordinary packing string, which can be found in any hardware store.

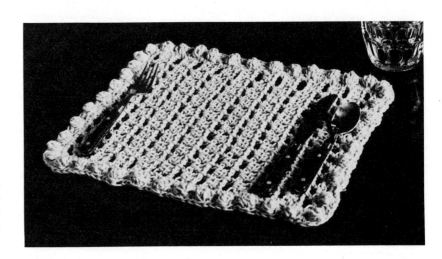

The combination of this soft ombré yarn and the dainty shell stitch give this pullover a very special look. Even beginners will find it very easy to make.

Teen Girls' Sizes

Directions are for size 10. Changes for sizes 12 and 14 are in parentheses.

Materials

8 (9, 10) skeins (1²/₅ oz or 40 g each) # 1 Country by Georges Picaud or any mohair to give gauge
1½ (1.4 m) yards elastic cord.

teen girl's
shell-stitch
pullover

Hook	**Gauge**
Size 10½ or K	3 shell stitches = 4 inches (10 cm)

Back

Chain 7.

Foundation row: Work 1 single crochet in 2nd chain from hook, 1 single crochet in each chain to end of row [6 single crochets].

Row 1: Chain 1 to turn, skip first stitch [chain-1 counts as first stitch], make 1 single crochet from back loop in next stitch, make 1 single crochet from back loop in each stitch to end of row.

Repeat row 1 for 40 (43, 46) rows.

Working along the long edge of border, work 1 single crochet in each row [40 (43, 46) single crochets].

Start shell pattern as follows:

Row 1: Chain 1, skip 3 stitches, *make 1 single crochet, chain 1, 1 single crochet all in next stitch, skip 2 stitches, repeat from * across row ending with 1 single crochet in last stitch [12 (13, 14) shells across row].

Row 2: Chain 1, turn, *make 1 single crochet, chain 1, 1 single crochet all in next chain-1 space, repeat from * across row, ending with 1 single crochet in top of turning chain.

Continue to repeat row 2 of shell pattern till 10 (11, 12) inches (25, 27.5, 30 cm), or desired length to underarm. Slip stitch over 1 complete shell pattern, work to within 1 pattern other side, chain, and turn. Continue to work on center 10 (11, 12) shells till armhole is 6 (6½, 7) inches (15, 16.3, 17.5 cm), end off.

Front

Work same as for back till armhole is 4 (4½, 5) inches (10, 11.3, 12.5 cm).

Shape neck as follows: Work across 2 (2, 3) shells, chain 1, and turn. Working on these 2 (2, 3) shells only, work till armhole is same as back to shoulder, end off. Skip the center 8 (9, 8) shells, join yarn at other side, and complete to correspond.

Sleeves

Chain 7. Work foundation row and row 1 same as for back. Repeat row 1 till 28 (28, 31) rows are worked. Working along long edge of border, pick up 1 single crochet in each row [28 (28, 31) single crochets]. Work shell pattern same as for back till sleeve is 15 (15½, 16) inches (37.5, 38.8, 40 cm), or desired length to underarm. Slip stitch over 1 shell pattern, work to within 1 pattern of other side, chain 1, turn. Working on the center 7 (7, 8) shells, work till cap is 6 (6½, 7) inches (15, 16.3, 17.5 cm). On next row, work single crochet, working 2 stitches together all across row, end off.

Finishing

Sew shoulder seams, set in sleeves. Sew underarm seams. Starting at right shoulder seam, work 3 rows single crochet around neck edge, pulling in slightly, if necessary. Run elastic through top of waistband and sleeve cuff. Do not block.

Boys' Sizes
One size fits all.

Materials
3 skeins (4 oz or 114 g each) Ambrosia 11 by Tahki, or any bulky yarn to give gauge

The colorful ombré yarn used for this hat and scarf set is fun to work with. The stripes automatically form as you're working, making interesting patterns. The yarn is very bulky, so the project works up very quickly.

boy's hat and scarf set

Hook	Gauge
10½ or K	2 stitches = 1 inch (2.5 cm)

Note: The hat is worked from the side over.

hat Body of Hat

Chain 25.

Foundation row: Work 1 single crochet in 2nd chain from hook, 1 single crochet in each stitch across row [24 single crochets].

Row 1: Chain 1, turn, skip 1 stitch [chain-1 always counts as first stitch], work 1 single crochet from back loop in next stitch, work 1 single crochet from back loop in each stitch to end of row [24 single crochets].

Row 2: Chain 1, turn, skip first stitch, work 1 single crochet from back loop in each stitch across row till last 6 stitches [do not work these stitches at this time] [18 single crochets].

Row 3: Chain 1, turn, skip first stitch, work 1 single crochet from back loop in each stitch to end of row [18 single crochets].

Row 4: Chain 1, turn, skip first stitch, work 1 single crochet from back loop on 18 stitches of previous row, plus work single crochet from back loop on 6 stitches previously skipped in row 2 [24 single crochets].

Repeat these 4 rows till piece measures 22 inches (55 cm) measured from the widest part, end off.

Finishing

Starting at bottom (widest part), sew 2 short ends together. Tie a knot, do not break yarn. Using same yarn that you sewed with, gather top, using small overcast stitches and picking up 1 stitch in each row, then pull to gather. Secure firmly, end off. Fold bottom up about 3 inches (7.5 cm) for border.

scarf Body of Scarf

Chain 17.

Foundation row: Work 1 single crochet in 2nd chain from hook, work 1 single crochet in each stitch to end of row.

Row 1: Chain 1 to turn, skip first stitch [chain-1 counts as first stitch], work 1 single crochet from back loop in each stitch to end of row.

Repeat Row 1 till 50 inches (125 cm) from beginning. Measure when slightly stretched, end off.

Finishing

Do not block.

To make fringe. Cut a piece of cardboard 6 inches (15 cm) long. Wind strands of yarn around it several times. Cut one end only. Take 2 strands of yarn just cut, fold in half. Using crochet hook, pull the 2 strands through a stitch, forming a loop about 1 inch (2.5 cm), then draw loose ends through loop. Continue to wrap yarn and fringe all around scarf, using 2 strands for each fringe.

Girls' Sizes
Directions are for size 8. Changes for sizes 10 and 12 are in parentheses.

Materials
2 (3, 3) skeins (1¾ oz or 50 g each) Windsor Cotton by Ulltex, or any cotton yarn to give gauge

Hook
Size 10 or J

Gauge
2½ stitches = 1 inch (2.5 cm)

Back
Chain 35 (37, 39).
Foundation row: Work 1 single crochet in 2nd chain from hook and 1 single crochet in each chain thereafter [34 (36, 38) single crochets].
Row 1: Chain 1 to turn, skip first stitch [chain-1 always counts as first stitch], make 1 single crochet in next stitch, make 1 single crochet in each stitch to end of row, make 1 single crochet in top of turning chain.

Repeat row 1, till piece is 8½ (9, 9½) inches (21.3, 22.5, 23.8 cm), or desired length to underarm, end off.

Straps
Starting in 7th (8th, 9th) stitch in from the edge, join yarn, and work single crochet on next 6 stitches, chain 1, and turn. Continue to work single crochet on these 6 stitches only for 6 (6½, 7) inches (15, 16.3, 17.5 cm), end off. Skip center 10 stitches and work 6 stitches to correspond for 2nd strap, end off.

Front
Work same as for back.

Finishing
Sew side seams, sew straps together at top. Do not block.

girl's cotton camisole

This little cotton camisole is a snap to make and fun to wear. It makes a terrific outfit when paired with the Girl's Lacy Jacket (see page 92).

girl's lacy jacket

Just the right weight for summer dressing, this lacy little jacket is made of a cotton yarn that is slightly heavier than most cotton yarns. The weight makes crocheting easier. Make it to go with the Girl's Cotton Camisole (see page 91).

Girls' Sizes
Directions are for size 8. Changes for sizes 10 and 12 are in parentheses.

Materials
9 (10, 11) skeins (1¾ oz or 50 g each) Windsor Cotton by Ulltex, or any cotton yarn to give gauge
5 buttons

Hooks
Size 10 or J

Gauge
2½ stitches = 1 inch (2.5 cm)

Back
Chain 41 (43, 45).
Foundation row: Work 1 single crochet in 2nd chain from hook, 1 single crochet in each chain thereafter [40 (42, 44) single crochets].
Row 1: Chain 3 *skip 1 single crochet, make 1 double crochet in next

92

stitch, make 1 double crochet in skipped stitch [1 cross stitch cluster made], repeat from * across row, ending with 1 double crochet in last stitch [you will have 19 (20, 21) clusters and 1 double crochet each side].

Row 2: Work same as for row 1.

Row 3: Chain 1, turn, skip first stitch [chain-1 counts as first stitch], make 1 single crochet in each stitch across row.

Row 4: Work same as for row 3.

Repeat these 4 rows for pattern. Continue in pattern till 8 (9, 10) inches (20, 22.5, 25 cm), or desired length to underarm, ending with Row 2 of pattern. Slip stitch over 4 stitches, work to within 4 stitches of other side, chain 1, turn. Next row, decrease 1 stitch each side [30 (32, 34) stitches remain]. Continue in pattern as established till armhole is 6 (6½, 7) inches (15, 16.3, 17.5 cm), end off.

Left Front

Chain 23 (25, 25). Work foundation row and row 1 same as for back. Repeat the 4 pattern rows same as for back to armhole. At arm side, slip over 4 stitches, work to end of row. On next row, decrease 1 stitch at arm side only. Keeping front edge even, continue in pattern as established until armhole is 4 (4½, 5) inches (10, 11.3, 12.5 cm), ending at front edge.

Shape neck as follows: Slip stitch over 8 stitches, being sure to keep pattern as established, decrease 1 stitch neck edge, every row, 3 (4, 3) times. Work on remaining 6 (7, 8) stitches to shoulder, end off.

Right Front

Work same as for left front, reversing all shaping.

Sleeves

Chain 31 (33, 35). Work foundation row and row 1 same as for back. Repeat 4 pattern rows till sleeve measures 10 (11, 12) inches (25, 27.5, 30 cm), or desired length to underarm, end with row 2 of pattern. Slip stitch over 3 stitches, work to within 3 stitches of other side, chain and turn. Continue pattern on remaining stitches till cap is 6 (6½, 7) inches (15, 16.3, 17.5 cm). End with row 2 of pattern. Next row, work single crochets, working 2 stitches together all across row, end off.

Finishing

Sew shoulder seams, set in sleeves, being sure to center gathered part on shoulder seam. Sew underarm seams.

To make border: Starting at right side seam, work single crochet along bottom to right corner, make 3 single crochets in corner stitch. Continue single crocheting up right front to top, make 3 single crochets in corner. Continue single crocheting along neckline to other side, make 3 single crochets in corner. Continue single crocheting down left front to bottom, make 3 single crochets in corner. Continue along bottom, back to where you started, join with a slip stitch. Make 2 more rows the same, making 5 buttonholes on 2nd row [right side] [to make buttonholes: chain 2, skip 1 stitch], on the 3rd row, work 1 single crochet in buttonhole chain. Do not block.

woman's mohair vest

Women's Sizes
Directions are for small size. Changes for medium and large sizes are in parentheses.

Materials
8 (9, 10) skeins (1¾ oz or 50 g each) of City Lights by Gemini, or any fluffy yarn to give gauge

Hooks
Size 6 or G
Size 10½ or K

Gauge
1 shell cluster = 1½ inches (3.8 cm)

Right Side
With larger hook, chain 65 (67, 79) loosely.

Foundation row: Starting in 4th chain from hook, make 2 double crochets, chain 1, 2 double crochets all in same stitch [shell cluster made]. *Skip 2 chains, work 2 double crochets, chain 1, 2 double crochets all in next stitch, repeat from * across row, ending skip 2 chains, make 1 double crochet in last chain [you will have 19 (20, 21) shell clusters and 1 double crochet each side].

Row 1: Chain 3, turn, make 2 double crochets, chain 1, 2 double crochets all in chain-1 space of first shell cluster of row below, *make 1 shell cluster in chain-1 space of next shell, repeat from * across row, ending with 1 double crochet in top of turning chain.

Repeat row 1 till piece measures 11 (11½, 12) inches (27.5, 28.8, 30 cm), end off.

Left Side
Work same as for right side.

Finishing
Lay 2 rectangles flat, with last shell row of each piece facing each other. Sew a seam 14½ (15, 15½) inches (36.3, 37.5, 38.8 cm) from one end [this forms back of garment]. Leave remaining section open for front. Fold piece in half, having seam just made as back, and sew 6 inches on each side, leaving remaining section open for armholes.

To make waistband: Use smaller hook and, starting at bottom left corner, with right side facing you, work 2 single crochets in each chain-2 space along bottom, ending at right front corner. Chain 1, turn. Continue to work in single crochet on these stitches for 2 inches (5 cm) end off.

To make ties: Using smaller hook and starting at bottom right side, with right side facing you, pick up 1 single crochet in each row of single crochet on waistband. Chain 1, turn. Continue to work single crochet on these stitches until tie is 12 inches (30 cm), end off. Starting at top of left waistband, make other tie to correspond, end off.

Using smaller hook, work 2 rows single crochet all around front and neck opening and all around armholes.

Do not block.

94

This easy-to-make vest simply consists of two rectangles joined together. The trick is to use a beautiful, exciting yarn to give it color and texture. The versatile vest can be worn over anything.

The rugged good looks of the homespun tweed and the shawl collar are sure to please any man. The yarn is used double strand, and the stitch is a simple one.

man's bulky tweed pullover

Men's Sizes
Directions are for size 36–38. Changes for sizes 40–42 and 44–46 are in parentheses.

Materials
12 (13, 14) skeins (3½ oz or 100 g each) Homespun Tweed by Tahki, or any yarn to give gauge

Hooks
Size 9 or I
Size 10½ or K

Gauge
2½ stitches = 1 inch (2.5 cm)
Note: Yarn is used double strand throughout.

see pages 74 (left) and 40 (right)

see page 76

see page 111

see page 96

see pages 65 (left) and 63 (right)

see page 81

see pages 47 (left) and 23 (right)

see page 156

see page 139

see pages 14 (left) and 131 (right)

see pages 124 (left) and 30 (right)

see page 87

see page 118

see page 155

see page 25

see page 102

see pages 49 and 51

see page 12

see page 45

see page 134

see page 67

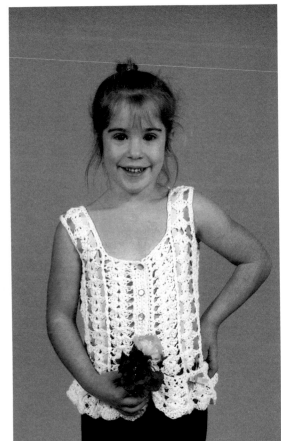

see page 106

see page 28

see page 27

see page 113

see page 122

see page 57

see page 135

see page 84

see pages 91 and 92

see pages 71 and 72

see page 9

Back

With smaller hook, chain 8.

Foundation row: Make 1 single crochet in 2nd chain from hook, make 1 single crochet in each chain to end of row [7 single crochets].

Row 1: Chain 1, turn, skip first stitch [chain-1 counts as first stitch], make 1 single crochet from back loop in next stitch, make 1 single crochet from back loop in each stitch to end of row.

Repeat row 1 for 50 (52, 54) rows. Working along long end of piece just made, pick up 1 single crochet in each row [50 (52, 54) single crochets]. Change to larger hook and work pattern as follows:

Row 1: Chain 1, turn, skip first stitch [chain-1 counts as first stitch] make 1 double crochet in next stitch, *make 1 single crochet in next stitch, make 1 double crochet in next stitch, repeat from * across row.

Row 2: Chain 1, turn, skip first double crochet, make 1 double crochet in next single crochet, *make 1 single crochet in next double crochet, make 1 double crochet in next single crochet, repeat from * across row.

Repeat row 2 until piece measures 15 (15½, 16) inches (37.5, 38.8, 40 cm), or desired length to underarm. Slip stitch over 2 stitches, work pattern till within 2 stitches of other side, chain and turn. Being sure to keep pattern as established, continue to work till 8½ (9, 9½) inches (21.3, 22.5, 23.8 cm) above armhole, end off.

Front

Work same as for back to armhole. Slip stitch over 2 stitches, work pattern on next 18 (19, 20) stitches, chain, and turn. Working on this section only, decrease 1 stitch at neck edge, every other row, 9 times. Work even on remaining 9 (10, 11) stitches till same as back to shoulder, end off. Skipping 10 stitches in the center, join yarn and work pattern on next 18 (19, 20) stitches. Finish to correspond to other side, end off.

Sleeves

With smaller hook, chain 8. Work foundation row and row 1 same as for back. Repeat row 1 for 32 (34, 36) rows. Working along the long end of piece just made, pick up 1 single crochet in each row [32 (34, 36) single crochets]. Change to larger hook and work pattern stitch same as for back, increasing 1 stitch each side [being sure to keep pattern], every 2½ inches (6 cm), 5 times [you should have 42 (44, 46) stitches]. Work even in pattern till sleeve measures 16½ (17, 17½) inches (41.3, 42.5, 43.8 cm), or desired length, end off.

Collar

With smaller hook, chain 11. Work foundation row and row 1 same as for back. Repeat row 1 till collar is 24 (25, 26) inches (59, 61.5, 64 cm), end off. Fold collar in half to find center, pin at center back of neck. Sew short ends of collar to bottom of neck opening, overlapping left over right. Now sew remaining sections of collar in place.

Finishing

Sew shoulder seams; sew side seams. Do not block.

three decorator pillows

aran isle pillow

Handmade pillows are fun and easy to make. The Aran Isle, Fluffy, or Geometric pillows would each make a wonderful gift because each can be made quickly and easily. The Aran Isle pillow is the only one that is really not for beginners.

Size
14 inches (35 cm) square

Materials
3 skeins (1²/₅ oz or 40 g each) Skol by Unger, or any yarn to give gauge
1 14-inch (35-cm) muslin pillow form.

Hook
Size N

Gauge
1½ stitches = 1 inch (2.5 cm)

Pattern
Row 1 (right side): Chain 5, skip 4 single crochets, make 1 single crochet in next stitch *chain 5, skip 3 single crochets, make 1 single crochet in next stitch, repeat from * across row.

Row 2: Chain 1, turn, *skip 1 stitch, holding loops to back of work, work 1 single crochet in each of next 3 single crochets, chain 1, repeat from * across row, ending with 4 single crochets.

Row 3: Chain 1, turn, skip 1 stitch, make 1 single crochet in each stitch and in each chain-1 space across row.

Row 4: Chain 1, turn, skip 1 stitch, make 1 single crochet in each stitch across row.

Row 5: Chain 1, turn, skip 1 stitch, make 1 single crochet in next stitch, catching loop into this single crochet, * 1 single crochet in each of next 3 single crochets, catch loop in next single crochet, repeat from * across row, ending with 2 single crochets.

Row 6: Chain 1, turn, skip 1 stitch, make 1 single crochet in each stitch across row.

Row 7: Chain 1, turn, skip 1 stitch, make 1 single crochet in each of next 3 single crochets, *chain 5, skip 3 single crochets, make 1 single crochet in next stitch, repeat from * across row.

Row 8: Chain 1, turn, skip 1 stitch, holding loops to back, make 1 single

98

crochet, chain 1 *1 single crochet in each of next 3 single crochets, chain 1, repeat from * ending with 2 single crochets.

Row 9: Repeat row 3.

Row 10: Repeat row 4.

Row 11: Chain 1, skip 1 stitch, make 1 single crochet in each of next 3 single crochets, *catch loop with next single crochet, make 1 single crochet in each of next 3 single crochets, repeat from * across, ending with 4 single crochets.

Row 12: Chain 1, turn, skip 1 stitch, make 1 single crochet in each stitch across row.

Row 13 (bobble row): Chain 1, turn, skip 1 stitch, make 1 single crochet in next stitch, *make 1 bobble in the next stitch [*to make a bobble;* make 5 double crochets all in same stitch, remove hook, place hook in first double crochet made in group, pull dropped loop through this double crochet], make 1 single crochet in each of next 3 single crochets, repeat from * ending with 1 bobble, 2 single crochets.

Row 14: Chain 1, turn, skip 1 stitch, make 1 single crochet in each stitch across row.

Repeat these 14 rows for 14 inches (35 cm) for pattern.

Note: Yarn is worked double strand throughout.

Front
Chain 25. Work pattern till 14 inches (35 cm) from beginning, end off.

Back
Chain 25.

Foundation row: Make 1 single crochet in 2nd chain from hook, 1 single crochet in each chain to end of row.

Row 1: Chain 1, turn, skip first stitch [chain-1 always counts as first stitch], make 1 single crochet in next stitch, 1 single crochet in each stitch to end of row.

Repeat row 1 for 14 inches (35 cm), end off.

Finishing
Holding back and front together, right sides out, and yarn double strand, work single crochet through both thicknesses around 3 sides of pillow, making 3 single crochets in each corner to turn. Insert muslin pillow inside this pocket, then crochet around 4th side, encasing muslin pillow into crocheted pillow. Join with slip stitch to first stitch. Working *backwards* over stitches just made, work another row of single crochet forming the raised backstitch border, end off.

fluffy pillow

Size
14 inches (35 cm) square

Materials
6 skeins (1^2/$_5$ oz or 40 g each) Aloha by William Unger, or any textured bulky yarn to give gauge

1 14-inch (35-cm) muslin pillow form

Hook   **Gauge**
Size P   1½ stitches = 1 inch (2.5 cm)

Note: Yarn is used double strand throughout.

Front
Chain 22.
Foundation row: Make 1 single crochet in 2nd chain from hook, 1 single crochet in each chain to end of row [21 single crochets].
Row 1: Chain 1, turn, skip first stitch [chain-1 counts as first stitch], make 1 single crochet in next stitch, 1 single crochet in each stitch to end of row.
    Repeat row 1 till front is 14 inches (35 cm) from beginning, end off.

Back
Work same as for front.

Finishing
Holding pieces, wrong sides together, and working through both thicknesses, work 1 row single crochet around 3 sides, making 3 single crochets in each corner to turn. Slip pillow form inside cover, and continue to single crochet along 4th side of pillow. Join with a slip stitch to first stitch, end off.

geometric pillow

Size
14 inches (35 cm) square

Materials
2 skeins (2 oz or 60 g each) Aspen by Brunswick, or any bulky yarn to give gauge

100

3 skeins (1¾ oz or 50 g each) Biancaneve by Fantacia, or any curly tweed to give gauge
1 14-inch (35-cm) muslin pillow form

Hook	**Gauge**
Size N	1½ stitches = 1 inch (2.5)

Front

With bulky yarn, chain 2.

Foundation row: Skip first chain, make 3 single crochets in 2nd chain.

Row 1: Chain 1, turn, make 1 single crochet from back loop in first stitch [chain-1 counts as first stitch, so that by making 1 single crochet in this stitch you are creating an increase], make 1 single crochet from back loop in next stitch, make 2 single crochets from back loop in last stitch [increase made]. [You will now have 5 single crochets in all.]

Row 2: Chain 1, turn, make 1 single crochet from back loop in first stitch, 1 single crochet from back loop in each stitch across row to last stitch, make 2 single crochets from back loop in last stitch [7 single crochets].

Continue to repeat row 2 until you have 33 stitches in all. Break off bulky yarn, join curly tweed, make 1 row single crochet from back loop all across row. Now, continuing to make single crochets from back loop, decrease 1 stitch at beginning and end of each row, until you have 1 stitch left, end off.

Back

Work same as for front.

Finishing

Holding pieces wrong sides together and working through both thicknesses, with bulky yarn work 1 row single crochet around 3 sides, making 3 single crochets in each corner to turn. Slip pillow form inside cover, and continue to single crochet along 4th side of pillow. Join with slip stitch to first stitch, do not end off. Work 1 row *backward* single crochet over stitches just worked, end off.

man's belted vest

Men's Sizes
Directions are for size 36. Changes for sizes 38 and 40 are in parentheses.

Materials
7 (7, 8) skeins (1¾ oz or 50 g each) Trenta by Angora Corporation of America, or any worsted weight yarn to give gauge
5 buttons
1 small buckle

Hook
Size 10½ or K

Gauge
2½ stitches = 1 inch (2.5 cm)

Back
Chain 43 (45, 47).
Foundation row: Make 1 single crochet in 2nd chain from hook, 1 single crochet in each chain to end of row [42 (44, 46) single crochets].
Row 1: Chain 1, turn, skip first stitch [chain-1 counts as first stitch], make 1 single crochet in next stitch, 1 single crochet in each stitch to end of row.

Repeat row 1, increasing 1 stitch each side, every 3 inches (7.5 cm), 3 times [48 (50, 52) single crochets]. Work even till 9 (9½, 10) inches (22.5, 23.8, 25 cm), or desired length to underarm. Slip stitch over 4 stitches, work to within 4 stitches of other side, chain and turn. Continue as established, decreasing 1 stitch each side, every row, 3 times [34 (36, 38) single crochets]. Work even till armhole is 9 (9½, 10) inches (22.5, 23.8, 25 cm), end off.

Left Front
Chain 2.
Row 1: Make 3 single crochets in 2nd chain from hook.
Row 2: Chain 1, turn [chain-1 counts as first stitch], make 1 single crochet in first stitch [this makes an increase], make 1 single crochet in next stitch, 2 single crochets in last stitch [this makes an increase] [you will have 5 single crochets].
Row 3: Chain 1, turn, make 1 single crochet in first stitch [increase], make 1 single crochet in each stitch to last stitch, 2 single crochets in last stitch [increase] [7 single crochets].

Continue to repeat row 3, increasing as established, until you have 23 stitches. Chain 1 (2, 3), turn. Working in new chain, work in single crochet all across row. Then chain 1 (2, 3) at end of row, turn. Working in the new chain, work all across row [25 (27, 29) stitches]. Work even until same as back to armhole, ending at arm side. Slip stitch over 4 stitches, finish row. Decrease 1 stitch at arm side, every row, 3 times and, at the same time, decrease 1 stitch at neck edge, every 3rd row, till 6 (7, 8) stitches remain. Work even till same as back to shoulder, end off.

Right Front
Work same as for left front, reversing all shaping.

Reminiscent of days gone by, the back-belted vest is fun and easy to make. We used a tweedy, textured yarn and a simple stitch.

Belt *(make 2 pieces)*
Chain 20 (22,24). Work foundation row and row 1 same as for back. Repeat row 1 for 1 inch (2.5 cm), end off.

Finishing
Sew shoulder seams, sew side seams.
  Work border as follows:
Row 1: Starting at right underarm seam at bottom, work single crochet down to point, make 3 single crochets in point. Continue along other side of point to bottom right front, make 3 single crochets in corner to turn. Continue up right front, all around neckline, down left front, make 3 single crochets in corner to turn, down to point, make 3 single crochets in point. Continue along bottom back to where you started, join with slip stitch in first stitch.
Row 2: Work same as for row 1, making 5 evenly spaced buttonholes on left front [*to make buttonholes*: chain 2, skip 1 stitch].
Row 3: Work same as for row 1, making 1 single crochet in each buttonhole, end off.
  Work 1 single crochet row around belts. Attach belt at side seams about 2 inches (5 cm) up from bottom. Sew buckle in place. Work 2 rows single crochet around each armhole, end off. Do not block.

103

teen girl's shell-cluster camisole

This crisp little camisole is just the thing to make you look and feel cool on a hot summer day. Made in cotton used double strand, and consisting of simple stitches, it can be made quickly and easily.

Teen Girls' Sizes
Directions are for size 10. Changes for sizes 12 and 14 are in parentheses.

Materials
15 (17, 18) balls (1 oz or 28 g each) Parisian Cotton imported by Joseph Galler, or any cotton yarn to give gauge
4 yards (3.6 m) grosgrain ribbon—2 yards (1.8 m) each in Colors A and B, ¼ inch (0.6 cm)
5 buttons

Hook   **Gauge**
Size 8 or H   3 patterns = 5 inches (12.5 cm)

Notes: Yarn is used double strand throughout.
  Camisole is worked from the top down.

Body
Chain 145 (153, 161).

104

Foundation row: Starting in 4th chain from hook, work 3 double crochets, chain 1, 3 double crochets all in same stitch [shell cluster made] *skip 3 chains, make 1 double crochet in next chain, make 1 shell cluster in next stitch, repeat from * across row, ending with skip 3 chains, 1 double crochet in last stitch [18 (19, 20) shells in all].

Row 1 [wrong side]: Chain 3, turn [counts as first double crochet], *make 1 shell cluster in chain-1 space from row below, make 1 double crochet under bar of next double crochet from back, inserting hook from right to left, picking up a loop, and completing as a double crochet, repeat from * across row, ending with 1 double crochet in top of turning chain.

Row 2: Chain 3, turn [counts as first double crochet], *make 1 shell cluster in chain-1 space of next shell, make 1 double crochet from front, under bar of next double crochet, inserting hook from right to left, pulling up a loop, and completing as double crochet. Repeat from *across row, ending with 1 double crochet in top of turning chain.

Repeat rows 1 and 2 till piece measures 9 (9½, 10) inches (22.5, 23.8, 25 cm), or desired length to underarm.

Work bottom flounce as follows:

Row 1: Chain 1, turn, *work 3 single crochets in space before next single crochet, work 3 single crochets in space before next double crochet, 1 single crochet in double crochet, repeat from * across row.

Row 2: Chain 3, turn, skip first stitch [chain-3 counts as first stitch], make 1 double crochet in next stitch, 1 double crochet in each stitch across row.

Row 3: Chain 3, turn, *skip 2 stitches, make a shell cluster in next stitch, repeat from * across row, ending with 1 double crochet in top of turning chain.

Row 4: Chain 3, turn, *make 1 shell cluster in chain-1 space of next shell, chain 1, repeat from * across, ending with 1 double crochet in top of turning chain.

Row 5: Chain 3, turn, *make 4 double crochets, chain 1, 4 double crochets in chain-1 space of next shell, chain 1, repeat from * across row, ending with 1 double crochet in top of turning chain, end off.

Straps

Foundation row: Joining yarn in 3rd double crochet in from end at top of garment, chain 3, make 1 shell cluster in center of next shell, make 1 double crochet in next double crochet.

Row 1: Chain 3, turn [chain-3 counts as double crochet], make 1 shell cluster in chain-1 space of shell, make 1 double crochet in double crochet.

Repeat row 1 till strap is 7 (7½, 8) inches (17.5, 18.8, 20 cm), end off. Skip 3 shells for underarm, join yarn, and work back straps to correspond.

Finishing

Sew straps at shoulder.

Work front border as follows:

Row 1 [left side]: Starting at top, work 1 row single crochet on left side.

Row 2: Chain 1, turn, work 1 single crochet in each single crochet. Repeat rows 1 and 2 once more, end off.

Row 1 [right side]: Starting at bottom of right side, work single crochet to top.

Row 2: Chain 1, turn, work 1 single crochet in each stitch.

Row 3: Chain 1, turn, work 1 single crochet in each stitch, making 5 evenly spaced buttonholes [*to make buttonholes:* chain 1, skip 1 stitch].

Row 4: Chain 1, turn, make 1 single crochet in each stitch and 1 single crochet in each chain-1 space of buttonholes.

Row 5: Chain 1, turn, make 1 single crochet in each stitch to top of right front, make 3 single crochets in last stitch, then continue with single crochet all along neckline, around straps, and back and down left front, making 3 single crochets at top of left front, end off.

Work 1 single crochet around armhole opening. Do not block. Run ribbon in and out opening at sides of shells as pictured. Tack ribbon at back and tie bows at bottom fronts.

girl's shell-cluster camisole

Girls' Sizes

Directions are for size 6. Changes for sizes 8 and 10 are in parentheses.

Materials

10 (12, 14) balls (1 oz or 28 g each) Parisian Cotton imported by Joseph Galler, or any cotton yarn to give gauge

4 yards (3.6 m) grosgrain ribbon—2 yards (1.8 m) each in Colors A and B, ¼ inch (0.6 cm)

5 buttons

Hook	**Gauge**
Size 8 or H	3 patterns = 5 inches (12.5 cm)

Notes: Yarn is used double strand throughout.
  Camisole is worked from the top down.

Body

Chain 97 (105, 113).

Foundation row: Starting in 4th chain from hook, work 3 double crochets, chain 1, 3 double crochets all in same stitch [shell cluster made] *skip 3 chains, make 1 double crochet in next chain, make 1 shell cluster in next stitch, repeat from * across row, ending with skip 3 chains, 1 double crochet in last stitch [12 (13, 14) shells in all].

Row 1 [wrong side]: Chain 3, turn [counts as first double crochet], *make 1 shell cluster in chain-1 space from row below, make 1 double crochet under bar of next double crochet from back, inserting hook from right to left, picking up a loop, and completing as a double crochet, repeat from * across row, ending with 1 double crochet in top of turning chain.

Row 2: Chain 3, turn [counts as first double crochet], *make 1 shell cluster in chain-1 space of next shell, make 1 double crochet from front, under bar of next double crochet, inserting hook from right to left, pulling up a loop, and completing as double crochet. Repeat from

106

*across row, ending with 1 double crochet in top of turning chain.

Repeat rows 1 and 2 till piece measures 6½ (7, 7½) inches (16.3, 17.5, 18.8 cm), or desired length to underarm.

Work bottom flounce as follows:

Row 1: Chain 1, turn, *work 3 single crochets in space before next single crochet, work 3 single crochets in space before next double crochet, 1 single crochet in double crochet, repeat from * across row.

Row 2: Chain 3, turn, skip first stitch [chain-3 counts as the first stitch], make 1 double crochet in next stitch, 1 double crochet in each stitch across row.

Row 3: Chain 3, turn, *skip 2 stitches, make a shell cluster in next stitch, repeat from * across row, ending with 1 double crochet in top of turning chain.

Row 4: Chain 3, turn, *make 1 shell cluster in chain-1 space of next shell, chain 1, repeat from * across, ending with 1 double crochet in top of turning chain.

Row 5: Chain 3, turn, *make 4 double crochets, chain 1, 4 double crochets in chain-1 space of next shell, chain 1, repeat from * across row, ending with 1 double crochet in top of turning chain, end off.

Straps

Foundation row: Joining yarn in 2nd double crochet in from end at top of garment, chain 3, make 1 shell cluster in center of next shell, make 1 double crochet in next double crochet.

Row 1: Chain 3, turn [chain-3 counts as double crochet], make 1 shell cluster in chain-1 space of shell, make 1 double crochet in double crochet.

Repeat row 1 till strap is 5 (5½, 6) inches (12.5, 13.8, 15 cm), end off. Skip 2 shells for underarm, join yarn, and work back straps to correspond.

Finishing

Sew straps at shoulder.

Work front border as follows:

Row 1 [left side]: Starting at top, work 1 row single crochet on left side.

Row 2: Chain 1, turn, work 1 single crochet in each single crochet.

Repeat rows 1 and 2 once more, end off.

Row 1 [right side]: Starting at bottom of right side, work single crochet to top.

Row 2: Chain 1, turn, work 1 single crochet in each stitch.

Row 3: Chain 1, turn, work 1 single crochet in each stitch, making 5 evenly spaced buttonholes [*to make buttonholes:* chain 1, skip 1 stitch].

Row 4: Chain 1, turn, make 1 single crochet in each stitch and 1 single crochet in each chain-1 space of buttonholes.

Row 5: Chain 1, turn, make 1 single crochet in each stitch to top of right front, make 3 single crochets in last stitch, then continue with single crochet all along neckline, around straps, and back and down left front, making 3 single crochets at top of left front, end off.

Work 1 single crochet around armhole opening. Do not block. Run ribbon in and out opening at sides of shells as pictured. Tack ribbon at back and tie bows at bottom fronts.

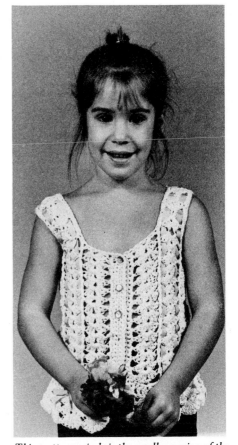

This pretty camisole is the smaller version of the Teen Girl's Shell-cluster Camisole on page 104. Together they make a lovely sister team.

man's classic v-neck cardigan

Men's Sizes
Directions are for size 36–38. Changes for size 40–42 and 44–46 are in parentheses.

Materials
9 (10, 10) skeins (4 oz or 114 g each) Ambrosia by Tahki, or any bulky yarn to give gauge
5 buttons

Hook
Size 10½ or K

Gauge
2½ stitches = 1 inch (2.5 cm)

Back
Chain 49 (53, 57).
Foundation row: Make 1 single crochet in 2nd chain from hook, 1

This classic V-neck cardigan takes on new dimensions when a bulky ombré yarn is used. The color changes create interesting patterns and texture. We used a bulky ombré and a large crochet hook to make this project fly.

single crochet in each chain to end of row [48 (52, 56) single crochets].

Row 1: Chain 1, turn, skip first stitch [chain-1 counts as first stitch], make 1 single crochet in next stitch, 1 single crochet in each stitch to end of row.

Rows 2–3. Repeat row 1.

Row 4: Chain 3, turn, skip first stitch [chain-3 counts as first double crochet], make 1 double crochet in next stitch, 1 double crochet in each stitch to end of row.

Repeat these 4 rows till piece measures 14 (14½, 15) inches (35, 36.3, 37.5 cm), or desired length to underarm. Slip stitch over 2 stitches, work to within 2 stitches of other side, chain, and turn. Continuing in pattern as established, decrease 1 stitch each side, every row, 3 times [there will be 38 (42, 46) stitches left]. Work even on the remaining stitches in pattern, till armhole is 9 (9½, 10) inches (22.5, 23.8, 25 cm) end off.

Left Front

Chain 24 (26, 28). Work foundation row and 4 pattern rows same as for back. Repeat 4 pattern rows same as for back to armhole, ending at arm edge. Slip stitch over 2 stitches, complete row. Continuing in pattern as established, decrease 1 stitch arm side, every row, 3 times, *and, at the same time*, decrease 1 stitch at neck edge every other row. Continue to repeat neck edge decrease until 10 (11, 12) stitches remain. Work even if necessary to shoulder, end off.

Right Front

Work same as for left front, reversing all shaping.

Sleeves

Chain 26 (28, 30). Work foundation row and 4 pattern rows same as for back. Continue to repeat 4 pattern rows, increasing 1 stitch each side, every 2½ (2½, 3) inches (6, 6, 7.5 cm), 6 times. Work even in pattern till sleeve is 17½ (18, 18½) inches (43.8, 45, 45.3 cm), or desired length to underarm. Slip stitch over 2 stitches, work to within 2 stitches of other side, chain, and turn. Continuing in pattern, decrease 1 stitch each side, every other row, till cap is 7 (7½, 8) inches (17.5, 18.8, 20 cm), end off.

Finishing

Sew shoulder seams, set in sleeves [when setting in sleeves, pin in place, easing in and rounding out at shoulder], sew underarm seams.

To make front border: Starting at bottom right front, work as follows:

Row 1: Working in single crochet, pick up stitches up right front, all around neckline, and down left front.

Row 2: Chain 1, turn, working in single crochet, make 5 evenly spaced buttonholes on this row [*to make buttonholes: chain 2, skip 1 stitch*], then continue all around same as for row 1.

Row 3: Repeat row 1, making 1 single crochet in each buttonhole space, end off.

Sew on 5 buttons. Do not block.

woman's ruffled blouse

Women's Sizes
Directions are for size 10. Changes for sizes 12 and 14 are in parentheses.

Materials
10 (11, 12) skeins (1¾ oz or 50 g each) Zig by Georges Picaud, or any silky yarn to give guage
1½ (1.4 m) yards elastic cord

Hook
Size 10½ or K

Gauge
3 shell stitches = 4 inches (10 cm)

Note: Yarn is used double strand throughout.

Back
Chain 43 (46, 49).
Foundation row: Starting in 3rd chain from hook, make 2 double crochets, chain 1, 2 double crochets all in same stitch, *skip 2 chains, make 2 double crochets, chain 1, 2 double crochets all in next stitch, repeat from * across row, ending with skip 2 chains, 1 double crochet in last stitch [12 (13, 14) shells].
Row 1: Chain 3, turn, make 2 double crochets, chain 1, 2 double crochets all in next chain-1 space of first shell, *make 2 double crochets, chain 1, 2 double crochets all in next chain-1 space, repeat from * across row, ending with 1 double crochet in top of turning chain.

Repeat row 1 till 10 (11, 12) inches (25, 27.5, 30 cm), or desired length to underarm. Slip stitch over 1 complete shell pattern, work to within 1 pattern other side, chain 3, and turn. Continue to work on center 10 (11, 12) shells till armhole is 6 (6½, 7) inches (15, 16.3, 17.5 cm), end off.

Front
Work same as for back till armhole is 2 inches (5 cm).
Shape neck as follows: Work across 2 (2, 3) shells, chain 3, and turn. Working on these 2 (2, 3) shells only, work till armhole is same as back to shoulder, end off. Skip center 6 (7, 6) shells, join yarn at other side, complete to correspond.

Sleeves
Chain 31 (31, 34). Work foundation row and row 1 same as for back. Repeat row 1 till 2 (2, 3) rows have been completed. Slip stitch over 1 shell pattern, work to within 1 shell pattern of other side, chain 3, turn. Working on the center remaining shells, work till cap is 7 (7½, 8) inches (17.5, 18.8, 20 cm). On next row, work single crochet, working 2 stitches together all across row, end off.

Finishing
Sew shoulder and side seams, set in sleeves.
To make neck ruffle: Starting at shoulder seam, work as follows:
Row 1: Single crochet all around neck, pulling in slightly, join with a slip stitch to first stitch.

A low, scooped neck and ruffles make this dainty blouse very dressy. We used a shiny yarn to add to its elegance.

Row 2: *Chain 6, skip 1 stitch, make 1 single crochet in next stitch from back loop, repeat from * all around, join with a slip stitch in first stitch.

Row 3: *Chain 6, make 1 single crochet in center of loop made by chain-6 from row below, repeat from * all around, ending with a slip stitch.

Row 4: Repeat row 3, end off.

Join yarn in same stitch that you began ruffle and work 3 more rows the same, working first row from front loop of single crochet row, end off.

To make sleeve ruffle: Repeat rows 1—4 of neck ruffle.

To make bottom ruffle: Repeat rows 1—4 of neck ruffle.

Run elastic through waist and sleeves. Do not block.

little girl's cotton jumper

Girls' Sizes
Directions are for size 4. Changes for sizes 5 and 6 are in parentheses.

Materials
6 (6, 7) skeins (1¾ oz or 50 g each) Windsor Cotton by Ulltex, or any cotton yarn to give gauge
1½ (1.4 m) yards satin ribbon, ¼ inch (0.6 cm)

Hook
Size 10 or J

Gauge
3 stitches = 1 inch

Back (Skirt)
Chain 71 (73, 75).
Foundation row: Make 1 single crochet in 2nd chain from hook, 1 single crochet in each chain to end of row [70 (72, 74) single crochets].
Row 1: Chain 3, *skip 1 single crochet, make 1 double crochet in next stitch, make 1 double crochet in skipped stitch [1 cross stitch cluster made], repeat from * across row, ending with 1 double crochet in last stitch.
Row 2: Repeat row 1.
Row 3: Chain 1, turn, skip first stitch, make 1 single crochet in each stitch across row.
Row 4: Repeat row 3.
   Repeat these 4 pattern rows till 8½ (9, 9½) inches (21.3, 22.5, 23.8 cm), or desired length to waist, ending with row 3 of pattern. Next row, work row 4, working 2 stitches together all across row [35 (36, 37) single crochets].
Next row: Chain 3, skip 1 stitch, *make 1 double crochet in the next stitch, chain 1, skip 1 stitch, repeat from * across row.
 Next row: Chain 1, turn, make 2 single crochets in each chain-1 space across row [35 (36, 37) single crochets].

Back Bodice
Continue to work single crochet on 35 (36, 37) single crochets for 3½ (4, 4½) inches (8.8, 10, 11.3 cm) more, end off.

Straps
Starting 9th stitch in from edge, join yarn and work across 6 single crochets, chain 1, turn. Work single crochet on these 6 stitches only for 3½ (4, 4½) inches (8.8, 10, 11.3 cm), end off. Skip center 7 (8, 9) stitches. Join yarn and work next 6 stitches to correspond, leaving remaining 8 stitches unworked.

Front
Work same as for back, except start straps on 7th stitch in from end and leave 11 (12, 13) in center.

Finishing
Sew straps at shoulders, sew sides seams. Work 1 row single crochet around armhole and neck. Run ribbon through open-work row at waistline and tie a bow in front. Do not block.

Little girls love pretty little dresses. We made this one in a soft cotton yarn, using a large crochet hook and simple stitches, making it easy to crochet.

Women's Sizes

Directions are for size 10. Changes for sizes 12 and 14 are in parentheses.

Materials

7 (8, 9) skeins (1¾ oz or 50 g each) Fluffy by Unger, or any other brushed yarn to give gauge
6 buttons

Hooks

Size 8 or H
Size 10½ or K

Gauge

2½ stitches = 1 inch (2.5 cm)

Back

With larger hook, chain 56 (60, 64) loosely.
Foundation row: Make 1 double crochet in 5th chain from hook, 1 double crochet in each of next 2 chains, now crossing back to 4th chain from hook, yarn over and pick up a long [at least 1 inch (2.5 cm)] loop, complete as a double crochet [1 cluster made]. *Skip 1 stitch, 1 double crochet in each of the next 3 stitches, 1 long double crochet in the skipped stitch. Repeat from * across, ending with 1 double crochet in last stitch, [13, (14, 15) clusters].
Row 1: Chain 3, turn, *skip first stitch, 1 double crochet in each of next 3 stitches, 1 long double crochet in skipped stitch, repeat from * across row, ending with 1 double crochet in last stitch.

woman's fluffy cross-stitch cardigan

The yarn used in this cardigan is a very soft brushed yarn that resembles mohair. It is light and airy to work with and makes a very delicate sweater. We made it in an interesting cross-over stitch that goes very quickly.

Repeat row 1 till 13½ (14, 14½) inches (33.8, 35, 36.3 cm), or desired length to underarm. Slip stitch over 3 stitches, chain 3, and continue pattern as established to last 3 stitches. Make a double crochet between last and next to last cluster to form a new end stitch [11 (12, 13) clusters], continue on remaining clusters till armhole is 7 (7½, 8) inches (17.5, 18.8, 20 cm), end off.

Left Front
With larger hook, chain 32 (32, 36) loosely.
Foundation row: Work same as for back.
Row 1: Work same as for back. There will be 7 (7, 8) clusters across row.

Continue to repeat row 1 till same as back to armhole, ending at arm side. Slip stitch over 3 stitches, chain 3, continue across row. Keeping pattern as established, work on remaining 6 (6, 7) clusters till armhole is 5½ (6, 6½) inches (13.8, 15, 16.3 cm), ending at front edge.

Shape neck as follows: Slip stitch over 4 clusters, chain 3, finish row. Continue to work on remaining 2 (2, 3) clusters till same as back to shoulder, end off.

Sleeves
With larger hook, chain 28 (28, 32).
Foundation row: Work same as for back.
Row 1: Work same as for back. There will be 6 (6, 7) clusters across row.

Continue to repeat row 1, increasing 1 stitch each side, every 2 inches (5 cm), 6 times, forming new clusters as enough stitches are increased. Work even till sleeve measures 14½ (15, 15½) inches (36.3, 37.5, 38.8 cm) or 1 inch (2.5 cm) shorter than desired finished length. Slip stitch over 3 stitches, chain 3, work pattern to within 3 stitches of other side, make 1 double crochet between last and next to last cluster to form a new end stitch, chain, and turn. Continue in pattern on remaining clusters till cap of sleeve is 7 (7½, 8) inches (17.5, 18.8, 20 cm). On next row, using smaller hook, work in single crochet, working 2 stitches together all across row, end off.

Finishing
Sew shoulder seams, set in sleeves. Sew underarm seams.
Work borders as follows:
Row 1: Starting at right seam, at bottom edge, using smaller hook, work single crochet all along bottom edge to right front, make 3 single crochets in corner. Continue up right front to neck, make 3 single crochets in corner. Continue around neckline, pulling in slightly if necessary, make 3 single crochets in corner. Continue down left front, make 3 single crochets in corner. Continue along bottom, back to where you started, join with a slip stitch in joining stitch.
Row 2: Repeat row 1.
Row 3: Repeat row 1, making 6 evenly spaced buttonholes on the right front [*to make buttonholes:* chain 2, skip 1 stitch].
Row 4: Repeat row 1, making 1 single crochet in each chain-2 buttonhole space.
Row 5: Repeat row 1, end off.

Work 5 rows single crochet around bottom of sleeves. Do not block.

Girls' Sizes
Directions are for size 8. Changes for sizes 10 and 12 are in parentheses.

Materials
11 (12, 13) skeins (1¾ oz or 50 g each) Viola by Unger, or any curly tweed to give gauge
2 spools (100 yds or 92 m each) Rayonette by Melrose, or any rayon yarn to give gauge
1 yard (1 m) elastic cord for tam
5 buttons

girl's gigot-sleeve jacket and tam set

This dressy jacket and hat would look terrific when paired with a matching skirt or worn over a dress. They are trimmed with a shiny rayon yarn that picks up one of the colors in the multiflecked tweed yarn that we used.

Hooks	Gauge
Size 10 or J	2 stitches = 1 inch (2.5 cm)
Size N	

Note: Yarn is used double strand throughout.

jacket

Back

With larger hook, chain 23 (25, 27) loosely.

Foundation row: Make 1 single crochet in 2nd chain from hook and 1 single crochet in each chain to end of row [22 (24, 26) single crochets].

Row 1: Chain 3, turn, skip first stitch [chain-3 counts as first double crochet], make 1 double crochet in next stitch, 1 double crochet in each stitch to end of row.

Repeat row 1, increasing 1 stitch each side, every other row, 3 times [28 (30, 32) double crochets]. Work even till 6½ (7, 7½) inches (16.3, 17.5, 18.8 cm), or 1½ inches (3.8 cm) less than desired length to underarm. Slip stitch over 2 stitches, work to within 2 stitches of other side, turn. Continue as established, decrease 1 stitch each side, every row, 2 times. Work even on remaining 20 (22, 24) stitches until armhole measures 6 (6½, 7) inches (15.5, 17, 18.5 cm), end off.

Left Front

With larger hook, chain 12 (13, 14) loosely. Work foundation row and row 1 same as for back. Continue to repeat row 1, increasing 1 stitch at arm side only, every other row, 3 times. Work even on remaining 14 (15, 16) stitches till same as back to armhole, ending at arm side. Slip stitch over 2 stitches, finish row. Continuing in pattern as established, decrease 1 stitch arm side, every row, 2 times. Work even on 10 (11, 12) stitches until armhole is 4½ (5, 5½) inches (11.3, 12.5, 13.8 cm), ending at neck edge. Slip stitch over 3 stitches, then decrease 1 stitch neck edge, every row, 2 times. Work on remaining 5 (6, 7) stitches till same as back to shoulder, end off.

Right Front

Work same as for left front, reversing all shaping.

Sleeves

With larger hook, chain 17 (18, 19) loosely. Work foundation row and row 1 same as for back. Continue to repeat row 1 till 9½ (10, 10½) inches (23.8, 25, 25.3 cm). On next row, work 2 double crochets in every stitch [32 (34, 36) double crochets]. Continue as established for 3 inches (7.5 cm) more. Slip stitch over 2 stitches, work to within 2 stitches of other side, chain, turn. Decrease 1 stitch each side, every row, 2 times. Work even till cap of sleeve is 5½ (6, 6½) inches (13.8, 15, 16.3 cm). On next row, change to size smaller hook and work 2 stitches together all across row [to work 2 stitches together, yarn over, pick up loop, yarn over and pull through 2 stitches, leave remaining loops on hook, insert hook into next stitch, yarn over, pick up a loop, yarn over and pull through 2 stitches, yarn over and pull through all stitches on hook], end off.

Finishing

Sew shoulder seams, set in sleeves by pinning in place first and easing puff, sew underarm seams.

To make border:

Row 1: With rayon yarn and smaller hook, starting at bottom right underarm seam, work single crochet along bottom to corner, make 3 single crochets in corner to turn. Continue up right front to neck, make 3 single crochets in corner to turn. Continue along top of neck, make 3 single crochets in corner to turn. Continue down left front, make 3 single crochets in corner to turn. Continue along bottom back to where you started, join with a slip stitch.

Row 2: Repeat row 1, do not break rayon yarn.

Row 3: With curly tweed yarn, repeat row 1, making 5 evenly spaced buttonholes, on right front [*to make buttonholes:* chain 2, skip 1 stitch], break curly tweed.

Row 4: With rayon yarn, repeat row 1, making 1 single crochet in each buttonhole space.

Row 5: Repeat row 1, end off.

Repeat same 5-row trim around bottom of sleeve.

Sew on buttons. Do not block.

Body of Tam

tam

With larger hook, chain 4, join with a slip stitch to form a ring.

Foundation row: Chain 3, make 11 double crochets in center of ring formed by chain-4.

Row 1: Chain 3, make 2 double crochets in each stitch around, join with slip stitch to top of chain-3.

Row 2: Chain 3, *make 1 double crochet in next stitch, make 2 double crochets in next stitch, repeat from * around, join with slip stitch to top of starting chain-3.

Row 3: Chain 3, *make 1 double crochet in each of next 2 stitches, make 2 double crochets in next stitch, repeat from * around, join with slip stitch to top of starting chain-3.

Continue to work in this manner, always having 1 stitch more between increases all around, until you have a 10-inch (25-cm) circle. Next row, change to larger hook and work 1 single crochet in each stitch.

Next row: Work in single crochet, decreasing every 7th and 8th stitch.

Next row: Work in single crochet, decreasing every 9th and 10th stitch, do not break curly tweed. Sew back seam. Change to rayon yarn, work 2 rows single crochet all around. Work 1 row single crochet with curly tweed, work 2 rows single crochet with rayon, end off.

Finishing

Run elastic through the rayon rows and pull in to fit head size.

woman's bulky coat

If you find you are always cold no matter what you wear, this coat is for you. It's wonderfully warm and bulky and fun to make. The yarn is variegated and creates its own pattern as you work.

Women's Sizes

Directions are for small size. Changes for medium and large sizes are in parentheses.

Materials

5 skeins (16 oz or 450 g each) Mardi Gras by Tahki, or any other bulky yarn to give gauge
5 large buttons

Hook   Gauge

Size P   1½ stitches = 1 inch (2.5 cm)

Notes: Garment is worked from side to side. Directions are for 39 (39½, 40) inches (97.5, 98.8, 100 cm) from shoulder to hem.

    This coat is a loosely fitted garment.

118

Back

Starting at side edge, chain 59 (60, 61) stitches loosely.

Foundation row: Make 1 single crochet in 2nd chain from hook, 1 single crochet in each chain to end of row [58 (59, 60) single crochets].

Row 1: Chain 1, turn, skip first stitch [chain-1 counts as first stitch], make 1 single crochet through back loop in next stitch, 1 single crochet from back loop in each stitch to end of row.

Repeat row 1 till piece measures 22 (22½, 23) inches (55, 56.3, 57.5 cm) wide, end off.

Left Front

Starting at side edge, chain 59 (60, 61) stitches.

Work foundation row and row 1 same as for back. Continue to repeat row 1 until 11 (11½, 12) inches (27.5, 28.8, 30 cm), end off.

Right Front

Work same as for left front.

Sleeves

Chain 26 (27, 28). Work foundation row and row 1 same as for back. Repeat row 1 till 17½ (18, 18½) inches (43.8, 45, 45.3 cm), end off.

Hood

Chain 22, work foundation row and row 1 same as for back. Continue to repeat row 1, increase 1 stitch at the end of the 4th row [mark this increase with colored thread]. Continue in pattern, increasing 1 stitch on same side as first increase every 4th row, 4 times more [mark last increase with colored thread]. Work even till 12 inches (30 cm) from beginning [mark here for center of hood]. Continue working even, until you are the same distance from the center marker to last increase marker, then decrease at this point. Continue in pattern as established to decrease 1 stitch every 4th row, 4 times more. Work 4 rows even, end off.

Finishing

Sew shoulder seams 5 (5½, 6) inches (12.5, 13.8, 15 cm) in from outside edge, leaving back of neck and remaining front stitches open. Sew side seams from bottom up, leaving 8½ (9, 9½) inches (21.3, 22.5, 23.8 cm) open for armhole. Fold sleeve in half and ease into armhole opening. Sew underarm seam. Fold hood in half and sew back seam. Center back seam at back of neck, pin edges of hood to front edges of coat, sew in place, easing in to fit.

To make front border: Starting at bottom right front, work single crochet up front, making 5 evenly spaced buttonloops, starting about halfway up from bottom [*to make buttonloops:* chain 3, skip 1 stitch] and ending at base of hood. Continue single crocheting all around hood and down left front, make 3 single crochets in corner, continue along bottom, end off. Fold hood back about 3 inches (7.5 cm).

Sew on buttons. Do not block.

child's summer cardigan

Child's Sizes
Directions are for size 2. Changes for sizes 3 and 4 are in parentheses.

Materials
7 (7, 8) skeins (1¾ oz or 50 g each) Swing by Unger—5 (5, 6) in Main Color, 1 in Color A, 1 in Color B—or any cotton yarn to give gauge
6 Buttons

Hook
10½ or K

Gauge
2½ stitches = 1 inch (2.5 cm)

Back
With Main Color, chain 31 (33, 35).
Foundation row: Work 1 single crochet in 2nd chain from hook, work 1 single crochet in each chain across row [30 (32, 34) single crochets].
Row 1: Chain 1, turn, skip first stitch [chain-1 always counts as first stitch], make 1 single crochet in next stitch, 1 single crochet in each stitch to end of row.

Repeat row 1, working 4 rows of Main Color, 2 rows of Color A, 2 rows of Color B, then continuing in Main Color until piece measures 8½ (9, 9½) inches (21.3, 22.5, 23.8 cm) from the beginning, or desired length to underarm. Slip stitch over 2 stitches, work to within 2 stitches of other side, chain, turn. Continuing as established, decrease 1 stitch each side, then continue till armhole is 4½ (5, 5½) inches (11.3, 12.5, 13.8 cm), end off.

Left Front
With Main Color, chain 16 (17, 18). Work foundation row and row 1 same as for back. Continue to repeat row 1, following striping pattern same as for back to armhole. Shape arm side same as for back. Keeping front edge even, work till armhole is 3 (3½, 4) inches (7.5, 8.8, 10 cm), ending at front edge.

Shape neck as follows: Slip stitch over 5 stitches, then decrease neck edge every row, 2 times. Work even on remaining 5 (6, 7) stitches until same as back to shoulder, end off.

Right Front
Work same as for left front, reversing all shaping.

Sleeves
With Main Color, chain 21 (22, 23). Work foundation row and row 1 same as for back. Continue to repeat row 1, following striping pattern same as for back till sleeve is 8½ (9, 9½) inches (21.3, 22.5, 23.8 cm), or desired length to underarm. Slip stitch over 2 stitches, work to within 2 stitches of other side, chain, and turn. Work even till cap of sleeve is 4 (4½, 5) inches (10, 11.3, 12.5 cm). On next row, work 2 stitches together all across row, end off.

Finishing
Sew shoulder seams, set in sleeves. Sew underarm seams.

This little cardigan, made with a textured cotton yarn, is just perfect for cool summer days. It's very easy to make and very easy to wear. Add contrasting color stripes for brightness.

Crochet border as follows:

Row 1: Starting at bottom right front, with Color A, work single crochet all along right front to neckline, make 3 single crochets in corner to turn. Continue around neckline, make 3 single crochets in corner to turn. Continue down left front, break off Color A.

Row 2: With Color B, starting at bottom right front, work a 2nd row of single crochet, making 6 evenly spaced buttonholes on this row, on the right side for girls, on the left side for boys [*to make buttonholes:* chain 2, skip 1 stitch], break off Color B.

Row 3: With Main Color, starting at bottom right front, work a 3rd row of single crochet, making 1 single crochet in each chain-2 space of buttonhole, end off.

Sew on buttons. Do not block.

teen boy's baseball cardigan

This cardigan is a little unusual as we have combined knitting and crocheting in one project. The borders and collar are knit in a ribbing stitch that is not difficult, and the sleeves are crocheted to form an interesting saddle shoulder.

Teen Boys' Sizes

The directions are for size 16. Changes for sizes 18 and 20 are in parentheses.

Materials

10 (11, 12) skeins (1¾ oz or 50 g each) Inverno by Fantacia, or any worsted yarn to give gauge
2 (2, 3) skeins (1²/₃ oz or 48 g each) Skol by William Unger, or any bulky yarn to give gauge
1 separating zipper

Hook	Knitting Needles	Gauge
Size 10½ or K	Size 8	5 double crochets = 2 inches (5 cm)

Note: Worsted yarn is used double strand, bulky yarn is used single strand throughout.

Back

With knitting needles and worsted yarn, cast on 68 (70, 72) stitches. Knit 1, purl 1 in ribbing for 3 inches (7.5 cm), bind off in ribbing, do not break yarn. With crochet hook, pick up 1 single crochet in every other stitch along bound-off edge of ribbing [34 (35, 36) single crochets].
    Work in pattern as follows:
Row 1: With worsted yarn, chain 2, skip first stitch [chain-2 counts as first stitch], make 1 double crochet in next stitch, 1 double crochet in each stitch to end of row.
Row 2: Repeat row 1, do not break yarn, but carry loosely up sides as you work.
Row 3: With bulky yarn, chain 1, make 1 single crochet in 2nd stitch from hook, 1 single crochet in each stitch to end of row.
Row 4: Work same as row 3, do not break yarn, but carry loosely up sides as you work.
    Repeat rows 1–4 for pattern. Work till 12 (12½, 13) inches (30, 31.3, 32.5 cm), or desired length to underarm. Slip stitch over 2 stitches, work to within 2 stitches of other side, chain, and turn. Decrease 1 stitch each side, every other row, 2 times. Work even till armhole is 6 (6½, 7) inches (15, 16.3, 17.5 cm), end off.

Left Front

With knitting needles and worsted yarn, cast on 34 (36, 38) stitches. Knit 1, purl 1 in ribbing for 3 inches (7.5 cm), bind off in ribbing, do not break yarn. Using crochet hook, pick up 1 single crochet in every other stitch on bound-off edge of ribbing [17 (18, 19) single crochets]. Work in pattern same as for back till same length as back to armhole. Shape arm side same as for back. Work even till armhole is 6 (6½, 7) inches (15, 16.3, 17.5 cm), end off.

Right Front

Work same as for left front, reversing all shaping.

122

Sleeves

With knitting needles and worsted yarn, cast on 40 (42, 44) stitches, work in knit 1, purl 1 ribbing for 3 inches (7.5 cm). Bind off in ribbing, do not break yarn. Pick up 1 single crochet in every other stitch along bound-off edge [20, (21, 22) stitches]. Using worsted yarn only throughout entire sleeve, but working pattern rows same as for back, increase 1 stitch each side, every 2½ inches (6 cm), 4 (4, 5) times. Work even till sleeve is 15½ (16, 16½) inches (38.8, 40, 41.3 cm), or desired length to underarm. Slip stitch over 2 stitches, work to within 2 stitches of other side, chain, and turn. Decrease 1 stitch each side, every other row, till 8 stitches remain. Work on remaining 8 stitches for 3 inches (7.5 cm) more [this forms saddle shoulder].

Collar

With knitting needles, cast on 73 (75, 75) stitches. Work in knit 1, purl 1 ribbing to last 3 stitches on row. Turn work around, do not work last 3 stitches. Slip 1 stitch, continue to work knit 1, purl 1 ribbing to last 3 stitches, turn, do not work last 3 stitches. Slip 1, knit 1, purl 1 in ribbing to last 5 stitches, turn, slip 1, rib to last 5 stitches, turn, slip 1, rib to last 7 stitches, turn, slip 1, rib to last 7 stitches, turn, bind off all stitches.

Finishing

Sew side seams, sew underarm sleeve seams. Starting at underarm, pin sleeves in place, having 3 inches (7.5 cm) of saddle on shoulder, between back and front sections. When you are sure sleeve is pinned in place properly, sew in. Center collar on back of neck, sew collar in place, having ends of collar reach ends of fronts.

Crochet border as follows:

Row 1: Using hook and worsted yarn and starting at bottom right corner, make single crochet along front edge to collar.

Row 2: Repeat row 1.

Row 3: Repeat row 1, end off.

Starting at top of left front, work same 3 rows of single crochet, end off.

Sew zipper in place. Do not block.

baby's yoked cardigan and hat set

Infants' sizes

Directions are for size 9 months. Changes for sizes 18 months and 2 years are in parentheses.

Materials

4 skeins (3½ oz or 100 g each) Germantown knitting worsted by Brunswick—2 skeins in Main Color, 1 skein each in Colors A and B—or any worsted weight yarn to give gauge
6 buttons

Hook

Size 10½ or K

Gauge

3 stitches = 1 inch (2.5 cm).

Pattern for Body

Row 1: Make 1 single crochet in each stitch across row.
Row 2: *Make 1 single crochet in next stitch, double crochet in next stitch, repeat from * across row.

Pattern for Yoke Divider

Row 1: Make 1 single crochet in each stitch across row.
Row 2: Chain 3 to turn, *skip 1 stitch, make 1 double crochet in next stitch, make 1 double crochet in skipped stitch, repeat from * across row.
Row 3: Make 1 single crochet in each stitch across row.

Pattern for Yoke

Row 1: Chain 1 to turn, make 1 single crochet in each stitch across row.

cardigan

Back

With Main Color, chain 32 (34, 36).
Foundation row: Work 1 single crochet in 2nd chain from hook, work 1 single crochet in each chain across row.

Work body pattern till 6½ (7, 7½) inches (16.3, 17.5, 18.8 cm), or desired length to underarm. Slip stitch over 2 stitches, work to within 2 stitches of other side, break off Main Color. Join Color A, work 3 rows of yoke divider pattern, break off Color A. Join Color B and work Row 1 of yoke pattern. Continue to repeat Row 1 of yoke pattern till armhole is 4½ (5, 5½) inches (11.3, 12.5, 13.8 cm), end off.

Left Front

With Main Color, chain 17 (18, 19). Work foundation row and row 1 same as for back. Continue to work same as back till armhole, ending at arm side. Slip stitch over 2 stitches, finish row, break off Main Color. Join Color A and work the 3 rows of yoke divider pattern, break off Color A. Join Color B, and work yoke pattern till armhole is 2½ (3, 3½) inches (6, 7.5, 9 cm) ending at front edge.

Shape neck as follows: Slip stitch over 5 stitches, decrease 1 stitch at neck edge, every row, 4 times. Work even on remaining 5 (6, 7) stitches till shoulder, end off.

Right Front

Work same as for left front, reversing all shaping.

Sleeves

With Main Color, chain 24 (26, 28). Work same as for back till yoke divider pattern has been completed. Join Color B and work even in yoke pattern till cap of sleeve is 4½, (5, 5½) inches (11.3, 12.5, 13.8 cm). On next row, work 2 stitches together all across row, end off.

Collar

With Color B, chain 32 (34, 36). Work Row 1 of yoke pattern. Continue in yoke pattern till collar is 2½ (2½, 3) inches (6, 6, 7.5 cm), end off.

Finishing

Sew shoulder seams, set in sleeves. Sew underarm seams. With Color B, work 1 row single crochet around 3 sides of collar, making 3 single crochets in corners to turn. Set collar aside. Do not sew on until front borders are crocheted.

To make front border:

Row 1: Starting at bottom right side, with Color B, work 1 row single crochet up to neck edge.

Row 2: Chain 1, turn, work a 2nd row of single crochet, making 5 evenly spaced buttonholes on this row if a girl's sweater. [*To make buttonholes:* chain 2, skip 1 stitch.]

Row 3: Chain 1, turn, repeat row 1, making 1 single crochet in buttonhole loops.

Make 3 rows single crochet on left front to correspond, making buttonholes on left side if a boy's sweater.

Center collar to back of neck, have edges of collar end halfway on front borders, sew in place. Sew on buttons. Do not block.

We used three colors and three different stitches to make this infant's cardigan and hat set. Make it in shades of blue for a boy, pretty pastels for a girl.

125

hat

Body of Hat

With Main Color, chain 41 (43, 45). Work foundation row and row 1 same as for back. Continue to work body pattern for 2½ (2½, 3) inches (6, 6, 7.5 cm), break off Main Color. Join Color A and work 3 rows of yoke divider pattern, break off Color A. Join Color B and work crown of hat as follows:

Row 1: Chain 1, turn, skip first stitch [chain-1 counts as first stitch], make 1 single crochet in each of next 4 stitches, work next 2 stitches together *make 1 single crochet in each of next 5 stitches, work next 2 stitches together, repeat from * across row.

Row 2: Chain 1, turn, skip first stitch, make 1 single crochet in each of next 3 stitches, work next 2 stitches together, *make 1 single crochet in each of next 4 stitches, work next 2 stitches together, repeat from * to end of row.

Row 3: Chain 1, turn, skip first stitch, make 1 single crochet in each of next 2 stitches, work next 2 stitches together, *make 1 single crochet in each of next 3 stitches, work next 2 stitches together, repeat from * to to end of row.

Row 4: Chain 1, turn, skip first stitch, make 1 single crochet in next stitch, work next 2 stitches together, *make 1 single crochet in each of next 2 stitches, work next 2 stitches together, repeat from * across row.

Row 5: Chain 1, turn, skip first stitch, work next 2 stitches together, *make 1 single crochet in next stitch, work next 2 stitches together, repeat from * across row.

Row 6: Chain 1, turn, skip first stitch *work next 2 stitches together, repeat from * across row, end off, leaving a long end for sewing.

First Earlap

Starting 1 inch (2.5 cm) in from edge, pick up 11 stitches along bottom of hat. Work body pattern for 4 rows. Then continue in pattern as established, decreasing 1 stitch each side, every row, till 3 stitches remain. Continue on 3 stitches for 5 (5, 5½) inches (12.5, 12.5, 13.8 cm). Chain 4, turn, skip 1 stitch, make 1 single crochet in last stitch, end off.

Second Earlap

Fold hat in half to determine where second earlap should start, then pick up 11 stitches and work to correspond to first earlap until 3 stitches remain, end off.

Finishing

Using end left at top of hat, gather top of hat and sew back seam. Starting at back seam, with Main Color, work 1 row single crochet along back, down earlap, down strap. Make 5 single crochets in loop at end of strap, continue around front of hat, around other earlap, making 3 single crochets in point of 2nd earlap. Continue back to where you started, join with slip stitch, end off. Make a pom-pom, if desired, for top of hat (see page 8 for pom-pom directions).

126

teen girl's flower-trim camisole

The feminine ruffles and the dainty flower trim make this camisole very special. It may look difficult, but it is really quite easy to make.

Teen Girls' Sizes

Directions are for size 10. Changes for sizes 12 and 14 are in parentheses.

Materials

14 (15, 16) skeins (10 oz or 284 g each) Parisian Cotton by Joseph Galler, or any cotton yarn to give gauge
6 small buttons
2 yards (1.8 m) flower trim or any dainty ribbon trim

Hook

Size 8 or H

Gauge

4 double crochets = 1 inch (2.5 cm).

127

Notes: Yarn is used double strand throughout.
Body is worked in one piece.

Body
Starting at waist, chain 136 (144, 152).
Foundation row: Starting in 4th chain from hook, make 1 double crochet in this chain, make 1 double crochet in each chain to end of row.
Row 1: Chain 3, turn, skip first stitch [chain-3 counts as first stitch), make 1 double crochet in each stitch to end of row.
Repeat row 1 till body is 8½ (9, 9½) inches (21.3, 22.5, 23.8 cm), or desired length to underarm, end off.

Straps
Join yarn 6 (6, 7) stitches in from edge, chain 3, work double crochet on the next 7 stitches, chain 3, and turn. Continue to work double crochet on these 8 stitches only for 14 (14½, 15) inches (35, 36.3, 37.5 cm), end off. Join yarn 14 (14, 15) stitches in from other side, chain 3, work double crochet in next 7 stitches, chain 3, and turn. Work double crochet on these 8 stitches only till same length as first strap. Leaving 19 (20, 21) stitches between for underarm, stitch end of strap to back.

Bottom Ruffle
Join yarn at bottom right corner, chain 4, work 2 triple crochets in each stitch along bottom. Chain 3, turn, work 1 triple crochet in each stitch along row. Chain 3, turn, skip 2 stitches, work 5 double crochets in next stitch, *skip 2 stitches, work 1 single crochet in next stitch, skip 2 stitches, work 5 double crochets in next stitch. Repeat from * across row, ending with skip 2 stitches, 1 double crochet in last stitch, end off.

Sleeve Ruffle
Join yarn at underarm, right side facing you, and repeat first and last row of bottom ruffle.

Borders
Starting at top left front, work 4 rows single crochet along left front edge, end off. Starting at bottom right front, work 4 rows single crochet along right front edge, making 6 evenly spaced buttonholes on 3rd row [*to make buttonholes:* chain 2, skip 1 stitch], then on 4th row, make 1 single crochet in button space, do not break yarn. Chain 1, turn, work a 5th row of single crochet up right front, make 3 single crochets in last stitch to turn, then continue single crocheting along top and all around straps and back, over to left front, make 3 single crochets in corner to turn. Continue down left front, make 3 single crochets in corner to turn, continue along bottom edge, making 3 single crochets in 3rd stitch of each shell along bottom. Continue back to where you started, join with a slip stitch, end off. Work 1 row single crochet around sleeve ruffle in same manner, end off.

Finishing
Sew flower trim along edge as shown. Sew on buttons. Do not block.

Women's Sizes

Directions are for size 10. Changes for sizes 12 and 14 are in parentheses.

Materials

10 (11, 12) skeins (1²/₅ oz or 40 g each) Dolly by Unger, or any other crinkly yarn to give gauge

9 (10, 10) skeins (⅓ oz or 10 g each) Angora by Angora Corporation of America, or any other angora to give gauge

Hooks	**Gauge**
Size 8 or H	3 shell stitches = 4 inches (10 cm)
Size 10½ or K	

Note: The crinkly yarn is used double strand, the angora is used single strand throughout.

Back

With larger hook and crinkly yarn, chain 43 (46, 49).

Foundation row: Starting in 3rd chain from hook, make 2 double crochets, chain 1, 2 double crochets all in the same stitch, *skip 2 chains, make 2 double crochets, chain 1, 2 double crochets all in next stitch. Repeat from * across row, ending with skip 2 chains, 1 double crochet in last stitch [12 (13, 14) shells].

woman's ruffled-neck cardigan

This very dressy cardigan has an angora ruffle at the neck; the same angora is used to make the sleeves, creating a very dramatic effect. Wear it for very dressy occasions.

Row 1: Chain 3, turn, make 2 double crochets, chain 1, 2 double crochets all in chain-1 space of first shell, *make 2 double crochets, chain 1, 2 double crochets all in next chain-1 space. Repeat from *across row, ending with 1 double crochet in top of the turning chain.

Repeat row 1 till 10 (10½, 11) inches (25, 25.3, 27.5 cm), or desired length to underarm. Slip stitch over 1 complete shell pattern, work to within 1 pattern other side, chain 3, and turn. Continue to work on center 10 (11, 12) shells till armhole is 6 (6½, 7) inches (15, 16.3, 17.5 cm), end off.

Left Front
With larger hook and crinkly yarn, chain 21 (24, 24). Work foundation row and row 1 same as for back [6 (7, 7) shells]. Continue to repeat row 1 till same as back to armhole, ending at arm side. Slip stitch over 1 complete shell pattern, work to end of row. Keeping pattern as established, continue to work on remaining 5 (6, 6) shells till armhole is 4 (4½, 5) inches (10, 11.3, 12.5 cm), ending at front edge. Slip stitch over 3 (4, 3) complete shell patterns, chain 3, and continue on remaining 2 (2, 3) patterns till armhole is same as back, end off.

Right Front
Work same as for left front, reversing all shaping.

Sleeves
With larger hook and angora yarn, chain 21 (22, 23).
Foundation row: Make 1 double crochet in 3rd chain from hook, 1 double crochet in each chain to end of row.
Row 1: Chain 3, turn, skip first stitch [chain-3 counts as first stitch], make 1 double crochet in next stitch, make 1 double crochet in each stitch to end of row.

Repeat row 1, increasing 1 stitch each side, every 3 inches (7.5 cm), 4 (5, 6) times. Work even till 16 (16½, 17) inches (40, 41.3, 42.5 cm), or desired length to underarm. Slip stitch over 2 stitches, work to within 2 stitches of other side, chain, and turn. Continue to work in double crochet, decreasing 1 stitch each side, every row, twice. Work even till cap of sleeve is 7 (7½, 8) inches (17.5, 18.8, 20 cm). On next row, make single crochets, making 2 stitches together all across row to gather top, end off.

Finishing
Sew shoulders, set in sleeves. Sew underarm seams.

To make ruffle and front border: Starting at bottom right front, with smaller hook and angora yarn, work 1 row single crochet up front to neck edge. Make 3 single crochets in corner stitch, then continue around neckline, pulling in slightly. Make 3 single crochets in corner stitch, continue down left front, end off.

Join yarn in the corner stitch at top right and *work ruffle as follows:* *Chain 8, skip 1 stitch, make 1 single crochet in front loop of next stitch, repeat from * to top of left front. Now, working along back loops of same stitches just worked, repeat from * back to where you started, join with a slip stitch, end off. Do not block.

130

toddler's sacque and hat set

This dainty little sacque is made from the neckline down. The yoke ruffles are added afterward and may be done in contrasting colors if desired.

Infants' Sizes
Directions are for 1 year. Changes for 2 years are in parentheses.

Materials
3 skeins (3½ oz or 100 g each) Reynolds Reynelle Knitting Worsted Orlon, or any worsted weight yarn to give gauge
3 buttons

Hook   **Gauge**
Size 6 or G   4 stitches = 1 inch (2.5 cm)

Note: Sweater is worked from the neck down.

131

sacque

Yoke

Chain 51.

Foundation row: Work 1 single crochet in 2nd chain from hook, 1 single crochet in each chain across [50 single crochets].

Row 1: Chain 1, turn, skip first stitch [chain-1 always counts as first stitch], make 1 single crochet from back loop in next stitch, 1 single crochet from back loop in each stitch to end of row. [*Note:* Entire yoke will be worked from the back loop.]

Row 2: Repeat row 1, increasing 1 stitch every 5th stitch [60 stitches].

Row 3: Repeat row 1.

Row 4: Repeat row 1, increasing 1 stitch every 6th stitch [70 stitches].

Row 5: Repeat row 1.

Row 6: Repeat row 1, increasing 1 stitch every 7th stitch (80 stitches).

Row 7: Repeat row 1.

Row 8: Repeat row 1, increasing 1 stitch every 8th stitch [90 stitches].

Row 9: Repeat row 1.

Row 10: Repeat row 1, increasing 1 stitch every 9th stitch [100 stitches].

Row 11: Repeat row 1.

Row 12: Repeat row 1, increasing 1 stitch every 10th stitch [110 stitches].

Row 13: Repeat row 1.

Row 14: Repeat row 1, increasing 1 stitch every 11th stitch [120 stitches].

This ends yoke part. Divide for body as follows:

Chain 3, turn, skip first stitch [chain-3 counts as first double crochet], make 1 double crochet in next stitch, 1 double crochet in each of next 18 stitches [these 20 stitches are 1 front], chain 3 (5), skip next 20 stitches [to be worked later for sleeve], work double crochet on next 40 stitches for back, chain 3 (5), skip next 20 stitches [to be worked later for sleeve], work remaining 20 stitches for front.

Working body all in one piece, work as follows:

Row 1: Chain 3, turn, skip 2 stitches, make 1 double crochet in next stitch, 1 double crochet in 2nd of skipped stitches *skip 1 stitch, make 1 double crochet in next stitch, 1 double crochet in skipped stitch, repeat from * across row, ending with 1 double crochet in last stitch.

Row 2: Chain 3, turn, skip first stitch, make 1 double crochet in next stitch, 1 double crochet in each stitch across row, 1 double crochet in top of turning chain.

Repeat rows 1 and 2 until 6 (6½) inches (15, 16.3 cm) from underarm, then *work ruffle as follows:*

Row 1: Chain 6, turn, skip 1 stitch, make 1 single crochet in next stitch *chain 6, make 1 single crochet in next stitch, repeat from * to end of row.

Row 2: *Chain 6, make 1 single crochet in loop of chain-6 from row below, repeat from * across row.

Row 3: Work same as for row 2, end off.

Sleeves

Join yarn in center of chain-3 (5) at underarm. Working in double crochet, work all around stitches reserved for sleeve, back to where you started, chain, and turn. Work in same pattern as body, working back and forth, till same length as body. Then work ruffle same as body, end off.

Yoke Ruffles
Starting at top, work ruffle on every other ridge formed by working single crochet from back loop. With right side facing you, join yarn in first stitch. *Chain 6, skip 1 stitch, make 1 single crochet in next stitch, repeat from * all around yoke, end off.

Finishing
To make front border:
Row 1: Starting at bottom of right front, work 1 row single crochet up front, make 3 single crochets in corner. Continue along top neckline, make 3 single crochets in corner. Continue down left front.
Row 2: Chain 1, turn, repeat row 1, making 3 evenly spaced buttonholes on yoke section [*to make buttonholes:* chain 2, skip 1 stitch.]
Row 3: Work same as for row 1, making 1 single crochet in each chain-2 of buttonholes.

Sew on buttons, sew underarm seam. Do not block.

Body of Hat   hat
Chain 45 (47).
Foundation row: Make 1 single crochet in 2nd chain from hook, 1 single crochet in each stitch across row.

Repeat rows 1 and 2 of body pattern for 4 (4½) inches (10, 11.3 cm), end off.

Back Section of Hat
Eliminating stitches on either side, work center 4 inches (10 cm) for 4 (4½) inches more (10, 11.3 cm), end off.

Sew back section to eliminated stitches.

Ties and Bottom Border
Row 1: Chain 45 (50) stitches. With right side facing you, join this chain to bottom corner of hat. Continue along bottom of hat with single crochet, pulling in slightly as you work. When reaching the other side, chain 45 (50) for other tie, turn.
Row 2: Chain 1, turn, work single crochet all along chain of 45 (50). Continue along bottom of hat, pulling in slightly. Then continue single crochet along first chain made, end off.

Finishing
Work 3 rows of bottom ruffle along front of hat, end off. Do not block.

girl's hat and scarf set

Sizes
One size fits all.

Materials
4 skeins (3½ oz or 100 g each) Brunswick Germantown Knitting Worsted—2 skeins in Color A, 1 skein each in Colors B and C—or any worsted weight yarn to give gauge

Hook	Gauge
Size 10 or J	1 shell pattern = 1¼ inch (3.1 cm)

Note: Do not break yarn after each row of color, but carry loosely up sides as you work.

scarf

Body of Scarf
With Color A, chain 33.
Foundation row: Starting in 3rd chain from hook, make 2 double crochets, chain 1, 2 double crochets all in same stitch [1 shell made], *skip 3 stitches, make 1 shell in next stitch, repeat from * all across row, ending with skip 2 stitches, 1 double crochet in last stitch [8 shells in all]. Continue to repeat row 1, alternating Colors A, B, and C, every 2 rows, till scarf is 60 inches (152.5 cm) long, end off.

Finishing
With Color A, work 1 single crochet along scarf edges, anchoring the carried-up yarn as you work the single crochet. Do not block.

This colorful hat and scarf are made with worsted yarn. Even though the stitch is slightly open, the scarf and hat are still warm and cozy.

hat

Body of Hat
With Color A, chain 60. Work foundation row and row 1 same as for scarf. Continue to repeat row 1 till 13 rows have been worked [there should be just 1 row of Color A shells on 13th row]. Next row, make single crochets, making 2 stitches together all across row, end off leaving a long thread for sewing.

Finishing
With long thread left at end of hat, gather top and sew back seam by weaving ends together to form a flat seam. With Color A, join yarn at seam and work 1 row single crochet all around bottom of hat, pulling in slightly to head size, end off. Turn bottom of hat up to form a brim. Fringe scarf with all leftovers.

To make fringe: Cut a piece of cardboard 8 inches (20 cm) long. Wrap yarn about 20 times around cardboard. Cut 1 end only. Take 2 strands of yarn just cut, fold in half. Using crochet hook, pull the 2 strands through a stitch, forming a loop about 1 inch (2.5 cm), then draw loose ends through loop. Continue to wrap yarn and fringe all around scarf, using 2 strands for each fringe.

134

Teen Boys' Sizes

The directions are for size 16. Changes for sizes 18 and 20 are in parentheses.

Materials

15 (16, 17) skeins (1¾ oz or 50 g each) Trenta by Angora Corporation of America, or any tweed yarn to give gauge
5 buttons

Hook

Size 10½ or K

Gauge

3 stitches = 1 inch (2.5 cm)

Back

Chain 51 (54, 57).
Foundation row: Make 1 single crochet in 2nd chain from hook, 1 single crochet in each chain to end of row [50 (53, 56) single crochets].
Row 1: Chain 1 to turn, skip first stitch [chain-1 counts as first stitch], make 1 single crochet in next stitch, 1 single crochet in each stitch to end of row.

Repeat row 1 till piece is 14 (14½, 15) inches (35, 36.3, 37.5 cm) from beginning, or desired length to underarm. Slip stitch over 3 stitches, work to within 3 stitches of other side, chain 1, and turn. Continue in pattern as established, decrease 1 stitch each side, every row, 2 times. Work even till armhole is 7½ (8, 8½) inches (18.8, 20, 21.3 cm), end off.

teen boy's shawl-collar cardigan

This easy-to-make, classic cardigan has the simple good looks that will please teenage boys. The interesting tweed yarn has great texture.

135

Left Front

Chain 26 (28, 30). Work foundation row and row 1 same as for back [25 (27, 29) single crochets]. Continue to repeat row 1 till armhole, ending at arm side. Slip stitch over 3 stitches, work to end of row. Continue to keep pattern as established, decreasing arm side, every row, 2 times, *and, at the same time,* decrease 1 stitch at neck edge every other row, till 8 (9, 10) stitches remain. Work even, if necessary, till same as back to shoulder, end off.

Right Front

Work same as for left front, reversing all shaping.

Sleeves

Chain 29 (30, 31). Work foundation row and row 1 same as for back [28 (29, 30) single crochets]. Continue to repeat row 1, increasing 1 stitch each side, every 3 inches (7.5 cm), 4 times. Work even till sleeve is 16 (16½, 17) inches (40, 41.3, 42.5 cm), or desired length to underarm. Slip stitch over 3 stitches, work to within 3 stitches of other side, chain 1, and turn. Continue to work in pattern as established decreasing 1 stitch each side, every other row, 9 (9, 10) times, end off.

Pockets *(make 2)*

Chain 18. Work foundation row and row 1 same as for back. Repeat Row 1 till pocket is 5 inches (12.5 cm), do not end off. With same yarn, work 1 row single crochet along sides and bottom of pocket, end off.

Front Border

Work 4 rows single crochet up to the start of V shaping on each front edge, making 5 evenly spaced buttonholes on the left front, in the 3rd row [*to make buttonholes:* chain 2, skip 1 stitch]. On 4th row, make 1 single crochet in buttonhole space, end off.

Collar

Chain 5, place a marker in last chain to mark end of row. Work foundation row and row 1 same as for back. Then continue to repeat row 1, increasing 1 stitch on the marked side only, every row, till there are 12 single crochets on collar. Place marker at end of last increase row. Work even in single crochet on 12 stitches till collar is 22 (22½, 23) inches (55, 56.3, 57.5 cm) from last marker. Then decrease 1 stitch on same side that you increased back to 4 stitches, end off.

Finishing

Sew shoulder seams. Sew collar in place, centering back of collar with back of neck and having ends of collar meet the top of the 4 crochet rows on each front. Set in sleeves, sew underarm seams. Sew on pockets. Starting at bottom right corner, work 1 row single crochets up front, all around collar, and down other side [this will make the 5th row of single crochet on fronts and 1 around collar], end off.

Sew on buttons. Do not block.

child's tweed vest

Interesting tweed yarn and a simple stitch make this little vest a sure winner. It can be made in a very short time and will please boys and girls alike.

Children's Sizes
Directions are for size 4. Changes for size 5 and 6 are in parentheses.

Materials
3 (3, 4) skeins (1¾ oz or 50 g each) Trenta by Angora Corporation of America, or any tweed yarn to give gauge
5 buttons
1-inch (2.5-cm) buckle for belt

Hooks
Size 8 or H
Size 10½ or K

Gauge
3 stitches = 1 inch (2.5 cm)

Back
With larger hook, chain 23 (25, 27).
Foundation row: Work 1 single crochet in 2nd chain from hook, 1 single crochet in each stitch to end of row [22 (24, 26) single crochets].
Row 1: Chain 1, turn, skip first stitch [chain-1 counts as first stitch], make 1 single crochet in next stitch, 1 single crochet in each stitch to end of row.

Repeat row 1, increasing 1 stitch each side every 1½ inches (3.8 cm), 3 times [28 (30, 32) single crochets]. Work even till 5½ (6, 6½) inches

(13.8, 15, 17.5 cm) from the beginning. Slip stitch over 2 stitches, work to within 2 stitches of other side, chain, and turn. Continue in pattern, decreasing 1 stitch each side, every row, twice. Work even on remaining 20 (22, 24) stitches until armhole is 5½ (6, 6½) inches (13.8, 15, 16.3 cm), end off.

Left Front
With larger hook, chain 2.
Foundation row: Make 3 single crochets in 2nd chain from hook.
Row 1: Chain 1, turn, make 1 single crochet in first stitch [because chain-1 always counts as first stitch, working in the first stitch after chain 1, rather than skipping it, makes an increase], make 1 single crochet in next stitch, 1 single crochet in each stitch until the last stitch, make 2 single crochets in last stitch [1 increase]. Continue to repeat row 1, making an increase in first and last stitch till you have 11 (13, 15) stitches on row. Work even for 1½ inches (3.8 cm), then increase 1 stitch at arm side. Continuing in pattern as established, repeat arm side increase, every 1½ inches (3.8 cm), 2 times more. Work even on the 14 (16, 18) stitches till same as back to armhole. Shape arm side same as for back, *and, at the same time,* decrease 1 stitch at neck edge, every other row, till 5 (6, 7) stitches remain. Work even till same as back to shoulder, end off.

Right Front
Work same as for Left Front, reversing all shaping.

Belt *(make 2)*
With larger hook, chain 18 (20, 22). Work foundation row and row 1 same as for back. Repeat row 1 for 1 inch (2.5 cm), end off.

Finishing
Sew shoulders, sew side seams. Tack belt pieces at side seams, approximately 3 inches (7.5 cm) up from bottom. Sew buckle to one end, thread other side through buckle.

Using smaller hook, and starting at bottom by seam, with right side facing you, *work border as follows:*
Row 1: Work single crochet along bottom of back, down front to point, make 3 single crochets in point. Continue up other side of point to bottom of right front, make 3 single crochets in bottom stitch. Continue up right front around neckline and down left front, make 3 single crochets in bottom stitch. Continue down to point, make 3 single crochets in point. Continue back to where you started, join with slip stitch to first stitch.
Row 2: Work same as for row 1, making 5 evenly spaced buttonholes on left front for boys, on right front for girls, [*to make buttonholes:* chain 2, skip 1 stitch].
Row 3: Work same as for row 1, making 1 single crochet in each chain-2 of buttonhole, end off.
Work 2 rows single crochet around each armhole.

Sew on buttons. Do not block.

Toddlers' Sizes
Directions are for size 1. Changes for sizes 2 and 3 are in parentheses.

Materials
4 (4, 5) skeins (1²/₅ oz or 40 g each) Dolly by Unger, or any other crinkly yarn to give gauge
3 buttons
4 yards (3.7 m) double-faced satin ribbon, ½ inch (1.3 cm)

toddler's party dress

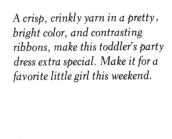

A crisp, crinkly yarn in a pretty, bright color, and contrasting ribbons, make this toddler's party dress extra special. Make it for a favorite little girl this weekend.

Hook	Gauge
Size 6 or G	3 double crochets = 1 inch (2.5 cm)

Note: Garment is started at waist; skirt part is worked from waist down. Bodice is picked up later and worked from waist up.

Skirt

Chain 103 (106, 109). Join with a slip stitch to form ring.
Foundation row: Chain 5, skip 2 stitches, make 1 double crochet in next stitch *chain 2, skip 2, make 1 double crochet in next stitch, repeat from * around, join with slip stitch to 3rd chain of starting chain-5 [34 (35, 36) open boxes].
Row 1: Chain 3 [this chain-3 counts as one-half of a V stitch], skip 1 open box, *make 1 double crochet, chain 1, 1 double crochet all in next open box, [this is a V stitch]. Repeat from * all around, ending with 1 double crochet in same stitch as starting chain-3. Chain 2, join with a slip stitch to tip of starting chain-3 [this completes another V stitch] [34 (35, 36) V stitches].

Note: Every row will begin with a half V stitch and end with half V stitch as established in row 1.
Row 2: Chain 3, *make 2 double crochets, chain 1, 2 double crochets all in chain-1 space of next V stitch [shell made]. Make 1 double crochet, chain 1, 1 double crochet all in chain-1 space of next V stitch [V stitch made]. Repeat from * all around, ending with 1 shell, 1 double crochet in chain-1 space of last V. Chain 1, join with slip stitch to top of starting chain-3.
Rows 3 and 4: Repeat row 2.
Row 5: Chain 3, *make 1 shell of 3 double crochets, chain 1, 3 double crochets all in chain-1 space of next shell. Make 1 V stitch in chain-1 space of next V stitch. Repeat from * all around, ending with 1 shell and 1 half V stitch. Join with slip stitch to top of starting chain-3.
Rows 6–10: Repeat row 5.
Row 11: Chain 3, *make 1 shell of 3 double crochets, chain 1, 3 double crochets in chain-1 space of next shell. Chain 1, make 1 V stitch in chain-1 space of next V stitch. Repeat from * all around, ending with 1 shell and 1 half V. Join with slip stitch to top of starting chain-3.

Repeat row 11, being sure to note that there is now a chain-1 before and after each V stitch, until skirt is 11 (11½) inches (27.5, 28.8 cm), or desired length from beginning, end off.

Bodice

Joining yarn at top back of skirt, chain 3 [chain-3 counts as 1 double crochet], work 0 (0, 1) double crochet in first open box, work 1 (2, 2) double crochet(s) in next open box, *work 2 double crochets in next open box, repeat from * 5 times more [14, (15, 16) double crochets worked over 8 open boxes].

Work left back bodice as follows on these 14 (15, 16) stitches:
Row 1: Chain 3, turn, skip first stitch [chain-3 counts as first double crochet], make 1 double crochet in next stitch, 1 double crochet in each stitch to end.

140

Row 2: Chain 5, turn, *skip 1 stitch, make 1 double crochet in next stitch, chain 2, repeat from * across, ending with 1 double crochet in last stitch.

Row 3: Repeat row 1.

Repeat rows 1–3 till bodice is 4½ (5, 5½) inches (11.3, 12.5, 13.8 cm), end off.

Right Back Bodice

Join yarn in 8th box over from center back of skirt, and complete as for left back bodice.

Front Bodice

Skip 1 open box for each underarm and work front on center 14 (15, 16) open boxes, picking up 2 double crochets in each box [28 (30, 32) double crochets]. Work as for left bodice, until 3 (3½, 4) inches (7.5, 8.8, 10 cm).

Shape neck as follows:

Work across 10 (11, 12) stitches, chain, and turn. Work in pattern as established, decrease 1 stitch at neck edge, every row, 3 times. Work even on remaining 7 (8, 9) stitches till same as back to shoulder, end off. Skip center 8 stitches, and work remaining 10 (11, 12) stitches to correspond.

Sleeves *(made from top down)*

Chain 31 (34, 37).

Foundation row: Starting in 3rd chain from hook, make a shell of 2 double crochets, chain 1, 2 double crochets all in same stitch, *skip 2 stitches, make 1 V stitch in next stitch, skip 2 stitches, make 1 shell in next stitch, repeat from * across row, ending with shell and 1 double crochet in last stitch.

Row 1: Chain 3, turn, *make 1 shell in chain-1 space of next shell, make 1 V stitch in chain-1 space of next V stitch, repeat from * across row.

Repeat row 1, till 7 (8, 9) rows made in all. At end of last row, chain 5, turn, form a new V stitch on chain-5, then continue pattern across, forming a new V stitch at the end of row in the same manner. Now work 2 more rows, making shells of 4 double crochets, chain 1, 4 double crochets, end off.

Finishing

Sew shoulders. Gather top of sleeve to form a puff, center on shoulder seam, then sew in sleeve. Starting at bottom right of the back opening, work single crochet up back, make 3 single crochets in corner. Continue around neck, make 3 single crochets in corner, continue down other side, chain 1, turn. Make a 2nd row of single crochet in same manner, making 3 buttonloops on right side [*to make buttonloops:* chain 4, make single crochet in same stitch]. Sew on buttons, run ribbon through open boxes on bodice front. Then run ribbon through waist, trying in front. Tie bows on bodice as desired. Run ribbon through bottom of sleeve, gather to desired length. Do not block.

141

teen boy's aran isle cardigan

Teen Boys' Sizes

Directions are for size 14. Changes for size 16 and 18 are in parentheses.

Materials

12 (13, 14) skeins (1²/₅ oz or 40 g each) Skol by Unger, or any other worsted weight yarn to give gauge
7 buttons

Hooks

Size 8 or H
Size 10½ or K

Gauge

2½ stitches = 1 inch (2.5 cm)

Note: Patterns are worked on fronts only.

Back

With smaller hook, chain 7.
Foundation row: Make 1 single crochet in 2nd chain from hook, 1 single crochet in each stitch across row [6 single crochets].
Row 1: Chain 1, turn, skip first stitch [chain-1 always counts as first stitch], make 1 single crochet from back loop in next stitch, 1 single crochet from back loop in each stitch to end of row.

This handsome Aran Isle Cardigan for teenage boys is not as difficult as it looks, but it really is not a beginner's project. It is a combination of three patterns made with a worsted weight yarn and a fairly large crochet hook.

Repeat row 1 till 40 (42, 44) rows have been worked in all [this completes bottom border]. Working along long end of border, pick up 1 single crochet in each row [40, (42, 44) single crochets]. Change to larger hook and continue to work in single crochet [through both loops] till piece measures 13 (13½, 14) inches (32.5, 33.8, 35 cm), or desired length to underarm. Slip stitch over 2 stitches, work to within 2 stitches of other side, chain 1, and turn. Continue in pattern as established, decrease 1 stitch each side, every row, 2 times. Work even on remaining 32 (34, 36) stitches until armhole is 7 (7½, 8) inches (17.5, 18.8, 20 cm), end off.

Left Front

With smaller hook, chain 7. Work foundation row and row 1 same as for back. Repeat row 1 till 20 (20, 24) rows have been worked. This completes front border. Working along the long end of border, pick up 1 stitch in each row across to last row. Pick up 2 stitches in last row [21 (21, 25) single crochets].

Change to larger hook and *work pattern on left front as follows:*
Row 1 (right side): Chain 5, skip 4 single crochets, make 1 single crochet in next stitch *chain 5, skip 3 single crochets, make 1 single crochet in next stitch, repeat from * across row [5 (5, 6) loops].
Row 2: Chain 1, turn, *skip 1 stitch. Holding loops to back of work, work 1 single crochet in each of next 3 single crochets, chain 1, repeat from * across row, ending with 4 single crochets.
Row 3: Chain 1, turn, skip 1 stitch, make 1 single crochet in each stitch and in each chain-1 space across row.
Row 4: Chain 1, turn, skip 1 stitch, make 1 single crochet in each stitch across row.
Row 5: Chain 1, turn, skip 1 stitch, make 1 single crochet in next stitch, catching loop into this single crochet, *make 1 single crochet in each of next 3 single crochets, catch loop in next single crochet. Repeat from * across row, ending with 2 single crochets.
Row 6: Chain 1, turn, skip 1 stitch, make 1 single crochet in each stitch across row.
Row 7: Chain 1, turn, skip 1 stitch, 1 single crochet in each of the next 3 single crochets *chain 5, skip 3 single crochets, 1 single crochet in next stitch, repeat from * across row [4 (4, 5) loops].
Row 8: Chain 1, turn, skip 1 stitch, holding loops to back, make 1 single crochet, chain 1 *make 1 single crochet in each of next 3 single crochets, chain 1. Repeat from *, ending with 2 single crochets.
Row 9: Repeat row 3.
Row 10: Repeat row 4.
Row 11: Chain 1, skip 1 stitch, make 1 single crochet in each of next 3 single crochets, *catch loop with next single crochet, make 1 single crochet in each of next 3 single crochets, repeat from * across, ending with 4 single crochets.
Row 12: Chain 1, turn, skip 1 stitch, single crochet in each stitch across.
Row 13 (bobble row): Chain 1, turn, skip 1 stitch, make 1 single crochet in next stitch *make 1 bobble in next stitch [*to make a bobble:* make 5

double crochets all in same stitch, remove hook, place hook in first double crochet made in group, pull dropped loop through this double crochet], make 1 single crochet in each of the next 3 single crochets. Repeat from *, ending with 1 bobble, 2 single crochets [5 (5, 6) bobbles in all].

Row 14: Chain 1, turn, skip 1 stitch, single crochet in each stitch across row.

Repeat these 14 rows for pattern. Work till same as back till armhole. Shape arm side same as back. Keep front edge even, being sure to keep pattern as established. Work till 5 (5½, 6) inches (12.5, 13.8, 15 cm) from armhole, ending at front edge.

Shape neck as follows: Slip stitch over 7 stitches, then decrease 1 stitch neck edge, every row, 2 (1, 4) times. Work even on remaining 8 (9, 10) stitches till shoulder, end off.

Right Front

Work same as for left front, reversing all shaping.

Collar

With smaller hook, chain 7. Work foundation row and row 1 same as for back. Continue to repeat row 1 for 38 (40, 42) rows, end off.

Sleeves

With smaller hook, chain 7. Work foundation row and row 1 same as for back. Continue to repeat row 1 for 22 (24, 26) rows. Working along long end of border, pick up 22 (24, 26) stitches. Change to larger hook and continue to work in single crochet [from both loops], increasing 1 stitch each side, every 2½ inches (6 cm), 5 times. Work even till 14½ (15, 15½) inches (36.3, 37.5, 38.8 cm), or desired length to underarm. Slip stitch over 2 stitches, work to within 2 stitches of other side, chain 1, and turn. Continue to work in single crochet, decreasing 1 stitch each side, every other row, 7 times, end off.

Finishing

Sew shoulders. Center straight part of top of sleeve on the shoulder seam. Sew in sleeve, easing and rounding cap as you sew. Sew under-arm seams.

Work front border as follows:

Row 1: Starting at bottom right side, work 1 row single crochet up to start of neck shaping.

Row 2: Chain 1, turn, skip first stitch, work 1 single crochet in each stitch to end of row.

Rows 3–5: Repeat row 2.

Starting at neck shaping on left front, repeat 5 rows of right front, making 7 evenly spaced buttonholes on 3rd row [*to make buttonholes:* chain 2, skip 1 stitch]. On 4th row, make 1 single crochet in each buttonhole space.

Fold collar in half, center on back of neck. Pin in place, having the ends of collar meet the top of each front border. Sew in place. Do not block.

144

Women's Sizes
One size fits all.

Materials
9 skeins (1/3 oz or 10 g each) 100% French Angora by Angora Corporation of America, or any angora to give gauge
1 yard (1 m) elastic cord

Hook	**Gauge**
Size 10½ or K	3 stitches = 1 inch (2.5 cm)

Body of Tam
Chain 4, join with slip stitch to first chain to form circle.
Foundation row: Make 8 single crochets in center of circle, place different color yarn at end of row and keep carrying this yarn down to use as a marker.
Row 1: Make 2 single crochets in each stitch around [16 single crochets].
Row 2: *Make 1 single crochet in next stitch, 2 single crochets in next stitch [increase made], repeat from * around to marker [24 single crochets].
Row 3: *Make 1 single crochet in each of next 2 stitches, 2 single crochets in next stitch [increase made], repeat from * around to marker [32 single crochets].
Row 4: *Make 1 single crochet in each of next 3 stitches, 2 single crochets in next stitch [increase made], repeat from * around to marker [40 single crochets].

Continue to increase every row, always having 1 stitch more between increases, until you have a 10-inch (25-cm) circle.
Work 3 rows even. Next row, decrease by working every 9th and 10th stitch together all around. Next row, decrease by working every 7th and 8th stitch together all round. Work even for 1 inch, end off.

Finishing
Run elastic through bottom and pull in to fit head size.

Body of Ascot
Chain 21.
Foundation row: Make 1 single crochet in 2nd chain from hook, 1 single crochet in each stitch to end of row [20 single crochets].
Row 1: Chain 1, skip first stitch [chain-1 always counts as first stitch], make 1 single crochet in next stitch, 1 single crochet in each stitch to end of row.

Repeat row 1 till 7 inches (17.5 cm). Next row, work 2 stitches together all across row [10 single crochets left]. Work on these 10 stitches for 14 inches (35 cm) *more.* Next row, increase 1 stitch in each stitch [20 single crochets]. Now work on these 20 stitches for 7 inches (17.5 cm) *more,* end off.

Finishing
Do not block.

woman's angora tam and ascot set

tam

Beautiful, fluffy angora was used to make this tam and ascot. It's an easy way to make a special gift for someone special or treat yourself to a touch of elegance.

ascot

toddler's aran isle pullover

Toddlers' Sizes
Directions are for size 2. Changes for sizes 3 and 4 are in parentheses.

Materials
6 (7, 7) skeins (2 oz or 60 g each) Silky Spun by Melrose, or any bulky yarn to give gauge
2 buttons

Hooks	Gauge
Size 8 or H	3 stitches = 1 inch (2.5 cm)
Size 10½ or K	

Note: Same pattern is used as Teen Boy's Aran Cardigan.

Pattern

Row 1 (right side): Chain 5, skip 4 single crochets, make 1 single crochet in the next stitch, *chain 5, skip 3 single crochets, make 1 single crochet in the next stitch. Repeat from * across row.

Row 2: Chain 1, turn, *skip 1 stitch, holding loops to back of work, work 1 single crochet in each of the next 3 single crochets, chain 1. Repeat from * across row, ending with 4 single corchets.

Row 3: Chain 1, turn, skip 1 stitch, make 1 single crochet in each stitch and in each chain 1 space across row.

Row 4: Chain 1, turn, skip 1 stitch, make 1 single crochet in each stitch across row.

Row 5: Chain 1, turn, skip 1 stitch, make 1 single crochet in the next stitch, catching loop into this single crochet, *make 1 single crochet in each of the next 3 single crochets, catch loop in the next single crochet. Repeat from * across row, ending with 2 single crochets.

Row 6: Chain 1, turn, skip 1 stitch, make 1 single crochet in each stitch across row.

Row 7: Chain 1, turn, skip 1 stitch, make 1 single crochet in each of the next 3 single crochets, *chain 5, skip 3 single crochets, make 1 single crochet in next stitch. Repeat from * across row.

Row 8: Chain 1, turn, skip 1 stitch, holding loops to back, make 1 single crochet, chain 1, *make 1 single crochet in each of the next 3 single crochets, chain 1. Repeat from *, ending with 2 single crochets.

Row 9: Repeat row 3.

Row 10: Repeat row 4.

Row 11: Chain 1, skip 1 stitch, make 1 single crochet in each of the next 3 single crochets, *catch loop with next single crochet, make 1 single crochet in each of the next 3 single crochets. Repeat from * across, ending with 4 single crochets.

Row 12: Chain 1, turn, skip 1 stitch, make single crochet in each stitch across row.

Row 13 (bobble row): Chain 1, turn, skip 1 stitch, make 1 single crochet in next stitch, *make 1 bobble in the next stitch [to make a bobble, make 5 double crochets all in the same stitch, remove hook, place hook in first double crochet made in group, pull dropped loop through this double crochet], make 1 single crochet in each of the next 3 single crochets. Repeat from *, ending with 1 bobble, 2 single crochets.

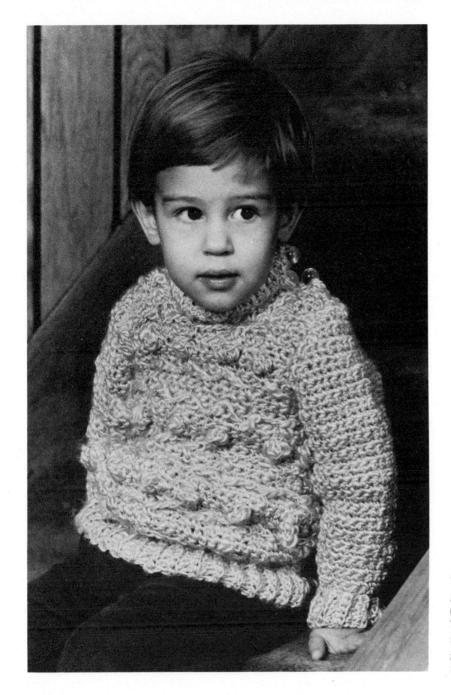

The same stitches that are used for the Teen Boy's Cardigan (page 142) are used in the Toddler's Aran Isle Pullover. We used a different yarn and used the pattern on the back as well as on the front.

Row 14: Chain 1, turn, skip 1 stitch, make 1 single crochet in each stitch across row.

Repeat these 14 rows for pattern.

Back

With smaller hook, chain 7.

Foundation row: Make 1 single crochet in 2nd chain from hook, 1 single crochet in each chain to end of row [6 single crochets].

Row 1: Chain 1, turn, make 1 single crochet from back loop in 2nd single crochet, 1 single crochet from back loop in each stitch to end of row.

147

Repeat Row 1 till 32 (36, 40) rows have been completed, [this completes back border].

Working along long end of border, pick up 1 stitch in each row across to last row, pick up 2 stitches in last row [33 (37, 41) single crochets]. With larger hook, work 14-row pattern till 8½ (9, 9½) inches (21.3, 22.5, 23.8 cm), or desired length to underarm. Being sure to keep pattern as established, slip stitch over 2 stitches, work to within 2 stitches of other side, chain 1, and turn. Decrease 1 stitch each side, once only. Work even till armhole is 4½ (5, 5½) inches (11.3, 12.5, 13.8 cm), end off.

Front

Work same as for back till armhole is 3 (3½, 4) inches (7.5, 8.8, 10 cm).
Shape neck as follows:
Work across 9 (10, 11) stitches, chain 1, and turn. Working on these stitches only, decrease 1 stitch neck edge, every row, twice, work to shoulder, end off. Skip center 9 (11, 13) stitches, work remaining 9 (10, 11) stitches to correspond, end off.

Sleeves

With smaller hook, chain 7. Work foundation row and row 1 same as for back. Continue to repeat row 1 till 18 (18, 20) rows have been worked [this completes sleeve border]. Working along long end of border, pick up 1 stitch in each row across [18 (18, 20) single crochets]. Change to larger hook. Continue to work in single crochet from both loops, increasing 1 stitch each side, every 1½ inches (3.8 cm), 4 times. Work even till sleeve is 8½ (9, 9½) inches (21.3, 22.5, 23.8 cm). Slip stitch over 2 stitches, work to within 2 stitches of other side. Continue to work in single crochet, decrease 1 stitch each side, every other row, 6 times, end off.

Collar

With smaller hook, chain 5. Work foundation row and row 1 same as for back till 30 (32, 34) rows have been worked, end off.

Finishing

Sew left shoulder only ½ inches (1.3 cm) in from edge, sew right shoulder. Center straight part of top of sleeve on shoulder seam, pin in place. Then sew sleeve in, easing and rounding the cap as you sew. Sew underarm seams. Sew collar in place, starting at left shoulder and centering on neckline. Work 1 row single crochet around opening at left shoulder, making 2 buttonholes on front [*to make buttonholes:* chain 2, skip 2 stitches]. Sew buttons in place. Do not block.

Size
Approximately 22 inches (55 cm) square

Materials
1 skein (2 oz or 60 g each) Dji Dji by Stanley Berocco, or any brushed wool to give gauge

2 skeins (⅓ oz or 10 g each) Angora by Angora Corporation of America, or any angora to give gauge

2 skeins (2 oz or 60 g each) Tiffany by Stanley Berocco, or any curly yarn to give gauge

4 skeins (1²/₅ oz or 40 g each) Aloha by William Unger, or any bulky textured yarn to give gauge

2 skeins (1²/₅ oz or 40 g each) Skol by William Unger, or any worsted weight yarn to give gauge

1 18-inch (45-cm) zipper

Hook
Size 10½ or K

Gauge
2 stitches = 1 inch (2.5 cm)

Note: All yarn is used double strand, except the bulky textured yarn.

Body of Bag
With bulky textured yarn, chain 45.

Foundation row: Make 1 single crochet in 2nd chain from hook, 1 single crochet in each chain to end of row [44 single crochets].

Row 1: Chain 1, turn, skip first stitch [chain-1 counts as first stitch], make 1 single crochet in next stitch, 1 single crochet in each stitch to end of row.

Rows 2−6: Repeat row 1, break off bulky textured yarn.

textured duffle bag

Here is a great big duffle bag to hold all your belongings. We used a combination of wonderful textured yarns in neutral colors, but it can be made just as effectively with any leftover yarn.

Rows 7 and 8: Join angora yarn. Repeat Rows 1 and 2. Break off angora yarn.

Rows 9–14: Join brushed wool yarn. Repeat rows 1–6. Break off brushed wool yarn.

Rows 15 and 16: Repeat rows 7 and 8.

Rows 17, 19, 21: Join worsted weight yarn. Chain 3, and turn. Make 1 puff stitch in first stitch [*to make puff stitch:* (yarn over hook, pick up a long loop) 3 times, yarn over hook and pull through all loops on hook] *chain 1, make 1 puff stitch in next stitch, repeat from * across row, ending with 1 double crochet in the last stitch.

Rows 18, 20, 22: With worsted weight yarn, chain 1, and turn. Make 1 single crochet in each chain-1 space across row, 1 single crochet in turning chain, break off worsted weight yarn.

Rows 23 and 24: Repeat rows 7 and 8.

Rows 25–30: Join curly yarn. Repeat rows 1–6. Break off curly yarn.

Rows 31 and 32: Repeat rows 7 and 8.

Rows 33–38: With bulky textured yarn, repeat rows 1–6. Break off bulky textured yarn.

Rows 39 and 40: Repeat rows 7 and 8.

Rows 41–46: Repeat rows 9–14, end off.

Side Circles (make 2)

With bulky textured yarn, chain 4, join with slip stitch to form circle.

Foundation row: Make 8 single crochets in center of circle, mark end of round using a different color thread, and carry marker down after each round.

Round 1: Make 2 single crochets in each stitch around [16 single crochets].

Round 2: *Make 1 single crochet in first stitch, 2 single crochets in next stitch, repeat from * around [24 single crochets].

Round 3: Make 1 single crochet in first 2 stitches, 2 single crochets in next stitch, *make 1 single crochet in each of next 2 stitches, 2 single crochets in next stitch, repeat from * around [32 single crochets].

Round 4: Make 1 single crochet in each of first 3 stitches, 2 single crochets in next stitch, *make 1 single crochet in each of next 3 stitches, 2 single crochets in next stitch, repeat from * around [40 single crochets].

Continue to work in this manner, increasing 8 stitches each round, and always having 1 stitch more between increases, until you have a circle that is 10 inches (25 cm) in diameter, end off.

Straps:

Using all your leftover yarn, make 2 twisted cords (see hints on page 8). Sew in place.

Finishing

Pin circles in place at each end of bag, using bulky textured yarn, single crocheting through both thicknesses all around. Sew sides of bag, inserting straps, leaving an 18-inch (45-cm) opening for zipper. Sew zipper in place.

Children's Sizes

The directions are for size 4. Changes for sizes 5 and 6 are in parentheses.

Materials

3 (4, 4) skeins (3½ oz or 100 g each) Reynelle by Reynolds—2 (3, 3) skeins in Main Color and 1 skein in Color A—or any worsted weight yarn to give gauge
6 (7, 7) buttons

Hooks
Size 8 or H
Size 10½ or K

Gauge
On Size 10½ hook, 3 stitches = 1 inch (2.5 cm)

Back

With Main Color and smaller hook, chain 33 (36, 39).
Foundation row: Make 1 single crochet in 2nd chain from hook, 1 single crochet in each stitch to end of row [32 (34, 36) single crochets].
Rows 1 and 2: With Main Color, chain 1, skip first stitch, [chain-1 always counts as first stitch], make 1 single crochet from back loop in next stitch, make 1 single crochet from back loop in each stitch to end of row, do not break Main color.
Rows 3 and 4: With Color A, repeat rows 1 and 2, do not break off Color A.

Repeat these 4 rows twice more, then, with Main Color, repeat rows 1 and 2. Break off Color A. Change to larger hook and continue to work single crochet through the whole stitch till 9 (9½, 10) inches (22.5, 23.8, 25 cm) from beginning, or desired length to underarm. Slip stitch over 2 stitches, work to within 2 stitches of other side, chain 1, turn. Continue to work as established, decreasing 1 stitch each side, every row, 2 times. Work even on remaining 24 (26, 28) stitches until armhole is 5 (5½, 6) inches (12.5, 13.8, 15 cm), end off.

Left Front

With Main Color and smaller hook, chain 18 (19, 20). Work foundation row and row 1 same as for back [17 (18, 19) stitches]. Continue to work same as for back till armhole. Shape arm side same as for back. Work even on remaining 13 (14, 15) stitches until armhole is 3½ (4, 4½) inches (8.8, 10, 11.3 cm), ending at front edge.

Shape neck as follows: Slip stitch over 3 stitches, then, continuing in pattern as established, decrease 1 stitch neck edge, every row, 3 times. Work even on remaining 7 (8, 9) stitches till same as back to shoulder, end off.

Right Front

Work same as for left front, reversing all shaping.

Sleeves

With Main Color and smaller hook, chain 18 (19, 20). Work foundation row and row 1 same as for back. Continue to work same as for back

This colorful cardigan can be worn by both boys and girls. The colorful striped borders and great big pockets are favorites of the young set.

until border is completed, break off Color A. Next row, increase 10 stitches evenly spaced across row [27 (28, 29) stitches]. Change to larger hook and work even till 9 (9½, 10) inches (22.5, 23.8, 25 cm). Slip stitch over 2 stitches, work to within 2 stitches of other side. Chain 1, turn, continue working in pattern, decreasing 1 stitch each side, every row, 2 times. Work even till cap is 5 (5½, 6) inches (12.5, 13.8, 15 cm), work 2 stitches together all across row, end off.

Collar

With Main Color and smaller hook, chain 38 (40, 42). Work foundation row and row 1 same as for back. Continue to work same as for back until border is completed, end off.

Pockets (make 2)

With Main Color and larger hook, chain 17 (18, 19).
Foundation row: Work 1 single crochet in 2nd chain from hook, 1 single crochet in each stitch to end of row [16 (17, 18) stitches].
Row 1: Chain 1, turn, skip first stitch [chain-1 always counts as first stitch], make 1 single crochet in each stitch to end of row.

Repeat row 1 till 2 (2½, 3) inches (5, 6, 7.5 cm) from beginning. Slip stitch over 8 (9, 10), stitches, work on remaining 8 stitches for 2 (2½, 3) inches (5, 6, 7.5 cm), end off.

Finishing

Sew shoulder seams. Center sleeve on shoulder seam, set in sleeve. Sew underarm seams. Center collar with center back of neck, pin in place, sew on collar. Sew on pockets, setting pocket right on top edge of border and right up to front edge of sweater.

Make border (right front) as follows:

Row 1: Starting at bottom right side, with Main Color and smaller hook, make single crochets along front edge, working through pocket along with front edge of garment, continue to neckline.
Row 2: Chain 1, turn, work in single crochet making 6 (7, 7) evenly spaced buttonholes on this row [*to make buttonholes:* chain 2, skip 1 stitch]. [If boy's, make buttonholes on left side.]
Row 3: Chain 1, turn, work 1 row single crochet, making 1 stitch in each chain-2 of buttonhole, end off.

Make border (left front) as follows: Starting at top of left front, make 3 rows of single crochet to match right front. (*Note:* If boy's sweater, make buttonholes on this side instead of right side.)

Do not block.

teen boy's loden jacket

This jacket is yet another example of how you can create a different look by combining a simple stitch with a great yarn and adding a few interesting touches.

Teen Boys' Sizes
The directions are for size 16. Changes for sizes 18 and 20 are in parentheses.

Materials
18 (20, 22) skeins (1²/₅ oz or 40 g each) Skol by William Unger, or any worsted yarn to give gauge
1 button
3 leather frogs

Hook   Gauge
Size 13   1½ stitches = 1 inch (2.5 cm)

Note: Yarn is used double strand throughout.

Back
Chain 29 (31, 33).
Foundation row: Work 1 single crochet in 2nd chain from hook, 1 single crochet in each chain across row [28 (30, 32) single crochets].
Row 1: Chain 1, turn, skip first stitch [chain-1 always counts as first stitch], 1 single crochet in next stitch, 1 single crochet in each stitch to end of row.

Continue to repeat row 1 till 15 (15½, 16) inches (37.5, 38.8, 40 cm), or desired length to underarm. Slip stitch over 2 stitches, work to within 2 stitches of other side, chain, and turn. Continuing in pattern as established, decrease 1 stitch each side, every row, 2 times. Work even on remaining 24 (26, 28) stitches till armhole is 7 (7½, 8) inches (18.8, 20, 21.3 cm), end off.

Left Front
Chain 18 (19, 20). Work foundation row and row 1 same as for back [17 (18, 19) single crochets]. Continue to repeat row 1 till same as back to armhole. Shape arm side same as for back. Keeping front edge even, work on remaining 15 (16, 17) stitches until armhole is 5 (5½, 6) inches (12.5, 13.8, 15 cm), ending at front edge. Slip stitch over 5 stitches, then, continuing in pattern as established, decrease 1 stitch neck edge, every row, 4 times. Work even on remaining 6 (7, 8) stitches till same as back to shoulder, end off.

Right Front
Work same as for left front, reversing all shaping.

Sleeves
Chain 18 (20, 22). Work foundation row and row 1 same as for back. Continue to repeat row 1, increasing 1 stitch each side, every 4 inches (10 cm), 3 times. Work even on 23 (25, 27) stitches till sleeve is 15½ (16, 16½) inches (38.8, 40, 41.3 cm), or desired length to underarm. Slip stitch over 2 stitches, work to within 2 stitches of other side, chain, and turn. Continuing in pattern as established, decrease 1 stitch each side, every 3rd row, 4 (4, 5) times, end off.

Collar
Chain 25 (27, 29). Work foundation row and row 1 same as for back. Continue to repeat row 1 till 5 inches (12.5 cm), end off.

Pockets *(make 2)*
Chain 13. Work foundation row and row 1 same as for back. Continue to repeat row 1 till 5 inches (12.5 cm) from the beginning, end off.

Finishing
Work 1 row single crochet around pockets. Work 1 row single crochet around 3 sides of collar. Sew shoulder seams. Sew underarm seams. Set in sleeves being sure to round out shape at shoulder. Center collar on back of neck, having edges of collar reach about 1 inch (2.5 cm) in from front edges. Starting at top of left front, with right side facing you, join yarn, chain 4, make 1 single crochet in next stitch, work single crochet along front edge, down to bottom, make 3 single crochets in corner, continue along bottom to other side, make 3 single crochets in corner, continue single crochet along right front, end off.

Sew button under collar on right side. Sew on leather frogs. Sew pockets in place. Do not block.

Size
36 inches (90 cm) square.

Materials
6 skeins (3½ oz or 100 g each) Zucca by Angora Corporation of America—3 skeins in Color A, 3 skeins in Color B—or any bulky yarn to give gauge
4 skeins (1²/₅ oz or 40 g each) Skol by Unger or any worsted weight yarn to give gauge

Hooks
Size 8 or H
Size N

Gauge
2½ stitches = 1 inch (2.5 cm)

Note: By combining the bulky and worsted yarns and by using different size hooks, a puffy texture can be achieved.

Square *(make 16)*
With larger hook and Color A, chain 2.
Foundation row: Make 3 single crochets in 2nd chain.
Row 1: Chain 1, turn, make 1 single crochet from back loop in first stitch [chain-1 counts as first stitch, so that by making 1 single crochet in this stitch, you are creating an increase], make 1 single crochet from back loop in next stitch, 2 single crochets from back loop in last stitch [increase made] [5 single crochets].
Row 2: Chain 1, turn, make 1 single crochet from back loop in first stitch, 1 single crochet from back loop in each stitch across row to last stitch, 2 single crochets from back loop in last stitch [increase made] [7 single crochets].

Continue to repeat row 2 until you have 19 stitches in all. Break off Color A, join Color B. Work 1 row single crochet from back loop all across row. Now, continuing to work single crochet from back loop, decrease 1 stitch at beginning and end of each row, until you are back to 1 stitch, end off.

Border
With smaller hook and worsted yarn, join yarn in any corner of square. Make 3 single crochets in corner, make single crochets all around, always making 3 single crochets in each corner, back to where you started, join with a slip stitch. Make a 2nd row all around, end off worsted weight yarn.

Finishing
Sew squares together, 4 across and 4 down. With smaller hook and worsted weight yarn, work 2 rows around entire outer edge of afghan in same manner of each square border.
Do not block.

child's brightly colored afghan

Having a brightly colored child-size afghan of his or her very own is sure to please any youngster. It's just perfect for cold winter evenings.

little girl's knickers and vest set

Girls' Sizes
Directions are for size 4. Changes for sizes 5 and 6 are in parentheses.

Materials
12 (12, 13) skeins (1¾ oz or 50 g each) Swing by Unger,—7 (7, 8) skeins for vest, 5 for knickers—or any nubby yarn to give gauge
5 (5, 6) buttons

Hooks
Size 8 or H
Size 10½ or K

Gauge
2½ stitches = 1 inch (2.5 cm) on the larger hook

vest

Back
With larger hook, chain 33 (35, 37).
Foundation row: Make 1 single crochet in 2nd stitch from hook, make 1 single crochet in each stitch to end of row [32 (34, 36) single crochets].
Row 1: Chain 1, turn, skip first stitch [chain-1 counts as first stitch], make 1 single crochet in next stitch, 1 single crochet in each stitch to end of row.

Continue to repeat row 1 till 2½ (3, 3½) inches (6, 7.5, 8.8 cm) from beginning. Then decrease 1 stitch each side and repeat decrease every 1½ inches (3.8 cm) 2 times more [26 (28, 30) stitches]. Work even for 2 inches (5 cm), then increase 1 stitch each side [28 (30, 32) stitches]. Work even till 10 (10½, 11) inches (25, 25.3, 27.5 cm), or desired length to underarm. Slip stitch over 2 stitches, work to within 2 stitches of other side, chain, and turn. Continue to work in pattern as established, decreasing 1 stitch each side, every row, 2 times. Work even till armhole is 5 (5½, 6) inches (12.5, 13.8, 15 cm), end off.

Left Front
With larger hook, chain 17 (18, 19). Work foundation row and row 1 same as for back [16 (17, 18) single crochets]. Continue to repeat row 1, shaping arm side same as for back, work to armhole. Shape arm hole same as for back and, *at the same time,* decrease 1 stitch neck edge, every other row, 7 times. Work even on remaining 5 (6, 7) stitches until same as back to shoulder, end off.

Right Front
Work same as for left front, reversing all shaping.

Finishing
Sew shoulder seams, sew underarm seams. Work 1 row single crochet around armholes. Before starting border, mark for 3 (3, 4) buttonholes, starting at waist up to neck shaping.
Make border as follows:
Row 1: Join yarn by right seam at bottom. Using smaller hook, work single crochets along bottom to right corner, make 3 single crochets in corner. Continue along right front up to neckline, continue around

156

Little girls love to dress up. This vest and knickers set paired with a pretty, feminine blouse will make any little girl the hit of the party.

neckline and down left front to bottom, make 3 single crochets in the corner stitch. Continue along bottom, back to where you started, join with a slip stitch to first stitch.

Row 2: Repeat row 1, making 3 (3, 4) buttonholes by markers [*to make buttonholes*: chain 2, skip 1 stitch].

Row 3: Repeat row 1, making 1 single crochet in each chain-2 space of buttonhole.

Sew on buttons. Do not block.

knickers

Right Side

With larger hook, chain 33 (35, 37). Work foundation row and row 1 same as for vest back [32 (34, 36) stitches]. Repeat row 1 for 6½ (7, 7½) inches (16.3, 17.5, 18.8 cm), or desired length from knee to crotch. Place a colored thread in work at this time to use for marker. Slip stitch over 2 stitches, work to within 2 stitches of other side, chain, and turn. Continue to work in pattern, decreasing 1 stitch each side, every row, 2 times. Work even on remaining 24 (26, 28) stitches till 7 (7½, 8) inches (17.5, 18.8, 20 cm), or desired length from crotch marker to waist, end off.

Left Side

Work same as for right side.

Finishing

Lay right and left sides on top of each other and sew a seam from waist to crotch marker on each side. These seams will be the front and back of garment. Place the garment so that the 2 seams just sewn will be lined up. Then sew leg seam from knee to crotch.

Turn right side out and *complete bottom of leg as follows*:

Starting at outside edge, make 1 row of single crochet along bottom of leg, pulling in slightly, back to where you started, do not join. Turn, and working back and forth along these stitches, make 4 more rows of single crochet. At end of last row, chain 4, and join in first row made, thus forming a buttonhole.

Sew button on each side. Do not block.

Using larger hook and yarn double strand, chain 100. Weave this chain in and out of the single crochet row at waistline to form a tie.

index

Make your home special

Since 1922, millions of men and women have turned to *Better Homes and Gardens* magazine for help in making their homes more enjoyable places to be. You, too, can trust *Better Homes and Gardens* to provide you with the best in ideas, inspiration and information for better family living.

In every issue you'll find ideas on food and recipes, decorating and furnishings, crafts and hobbies, remodeling and building, gardening and outdoor living plus family money management, health, education, pets, car maintenance and more.

For information on how you can have *Better Homes and Gardens* delivered to your door, write to: Mr. Robert Austin, P.O. Box 4536, Des Moines, IA 50336.

Better Homes ®
and Gardens

*The Idea Magazine
for Better Homes
and Families*